MW01442456

Beyond the Sand and Sea

A poetic anthology inspired by the sea, seashore, lighthouses, and anything associated with life on or near the sea.

Paul Gilliland

Editor-in-Chief

Southern Arizona Press

Southern Arizona Press

Southern Arizona Press

The mission of Southern Arizona Press is to promote the works of self-published and lesser-known unpublished authors and poets to the rest of the world through publishing themed and unthemed anthologies and assisting in the publication and promotion of their works.

It is our desire to make the voices of these aspiring poets and authors available to as wide an audience as possible with the belief that no writer of poetry or literature should ever have to pay to have their works published.

Beyond the Sand and Sea

All rights reserved. Copyright © 2023 by Paul Gilliland and Southern Arizona Press. Except as permitted under the Copyright Act of 1976, no portion of this book may be reproduced or distributed in any form, or by any means without prior written consent of the individual authors or the publisher. Individual works Copyright © retained by the poetic author. Previously published works have been cited and each publication acknowledged to the best of our ability. If any citations have been missed, such errors will be corrected in subsequent reprints.

If you would like your work to be considered for future anthologies, please visit us at:
http://www.southernarizonapress.com/current-submissions/
for a full list of current open anthology submissions and submission guidelines.

Published by Southern Arizona Press
Sierra Vista, Arizona 85635
www.southernarizonapress.com

Follow us on Facebook at:
https://www.facebook.com/SouthernArizonaPress

Format, cover design, and edits by Paul Gilliland, Editor-in-Chief, Southern Arizona Press

Cover Art: *Beach* – Image by Ernesto Velázquez from Pixabay
Interior Art: As noted from Pixabay

Poets photos Copyright © retained by submitting poets

ISBN: 9781960038340

Table of Contents

Featured Poet

Carol Edwards is a mostly self-taught poet from northern California transplanted to southern Arizona. She lives and works in relative seclusion with her books, plants, and pets (2 dogs, 5 cats, + husband). She grew up reading fantasy and classic novels, climbing trees, and acquiring frequent grass stains. She enjoys a coffee addiction, raising her succulent army, and volunteering at local pop culture and literary conventions. A few of her favorite places to visit, in the rare instances she can, are Noyo Headlands Park in Fort Bragg, California; Mendocino Headlands State Park in Mendocino, California; Samoa Beach in Eureka, California; Cannon Beach, Oregon; and Whidbey Island, Washington.

She won "Best in Collection" for her poems in *Balm 2* (The Ravens Quoth Press, 2022). She is a member of the Science Fiction & Fantasy Poetry Association (SFPA).

Her work has appeared in myriad publications and anthologies since early 2020, both online and in print, including *Space & Time*; *Where You'll Find Me* (a mini-chapbook from Origami Poems Project, 2020); *Uproar*, a literary Blog by The Lawrence House Centre for the Arts; *Heart of Flesh Literary Journal*; Cajun Mutt Press; *Agape Review*; *the ocean waves, the leaves fall*, *Words for the Earth*, and *Where Flowers Bloom* (Red Penguin Books, 2021-2022); *Open Skies Quarterly*; *Otherwise Engaged Literary and Art Journal*; *Trouvaille Review*; *POETiCA REViEW*; *Panoply Zine*; *Balm 2*, *Cherish*, *Tempest*, *Evermore 2*, and *Dream 2* (The Ravens Quoth Press, 2022-2023); *The Stars and Moon in the Evening Sky*, *Dragonflies and Fairies*, *The Wonders of Winter*, and *Love Letters in Poetic Verse* (Southern Arizona Press 2022 -2023); *#Aeration* and *#GroundingEarth* (White Stag Publishing, 2022); *The Post Grad Journal*; and the Detroit Lakes 2023 Poetry Walk in Detroit Lakes, Minnesota.

More of her poems are forthcoming in *#SPIRIT* (White Stag Publishing, October 2023) and in *UNDER HER EYE* (Black Spot Books, November 2023).

Her debut poetry collection, *The World Eats Love*, released April 25, 2023 from The Ravens Quoth Press in e-book and print versions: https://books2read.com/TWEL-by-Carol-Edwards

She sporadically uploads her poetry to her blog https://practicallypoetical.wordpress.com.

IG: @practicallypoetical
Facebook/Twitter: @practicallypoet

Driftwood Dryad

I hold the sky and see in my hands
feel the heartbeat of Earth in sands.
I hear the song of your raging,
bend to the power of your wind,
my skin scraped clean,
my green
long since dimmed.
Your salt spray scours my bones,
twisted, gnarled, stripped;
beautiful I am not,
save on nights
when I and my sisters tripped
whispered steps in silv'ry light
your waves glimmering,
gossamer veils both gowns and shrouds,
stone-pale tresses billowed crowns
until daybreak, when the spell drowns.

Previously published in *the ocean waves*, Red Penguin Books, 2021

Tucked in a Timber Throne at the Edge of the World

Sitting at the headlands
one-eighty ocean view
I feel compelled to proselytize
to leave unwasted these precious few
minutes for which I endured thousands;
but I don't feel inspired
just tired
my cup barely floating dregs
cracked from lip to base
leaking joy's cordial onto barren sands
thirsty in their own right
de-hydrated by a saline waste
an eighth mile distant.
But the sea speaks not to me
of pains and patience
and sleeplessness;
rather, like far distant friends
resume where they left off
a decade since
and in each other's presence
regain a comfort they nearly forgot,
she sings and sighs to me
a soothing purr of Blues,
a salve to long-suffered wounds.

Previously published in *the ocean waves*, Red Penguin Books, 2021

Drop-off

I feel safer from high enough away,
no sand to scrape soft places
or fold in the arches of my feet,
no renegade waves to plow
headfirst into my precarious perch
that juts to meet the soothingly
violent surf because it's broody
and romantic
and close, so close, but far enough
to keep from soaking jeans and shoes
lest my skin be doomed to chafe raw
in the long traipse back to the car,

no kelp to brush bare ankles
and bring to mind vividly terrifying
anecdotes my cousins told
of people tangled with stinging jellyfish
or rabid monster eels, or sharks
in a bloodlust rage charging all the way to shore
over a split heel, a scraped toe,
no carnivorous fanged fish or beaked
cephalopod lurking just past the drop-off
craving taste of woman-flesh,
and no riptide to drag me by the knees
into an undertow and out to sea
where I'd either suffocate
crushed to the ocean floor

or dehydrate
in an endless saline waste, the sun
slow sucking moisture out, like I'm
a bastille and it must mercilessly
wrestle captives free
drop. by. drop.
until naught but a corse remains
bones and bloated flesh
adrift on murky tides,
waves of blue despoiled by
iridescent oils coiled with
glaring polystyrene islands,
beaks and teeth exacting their pounds of flesh
for the debts of violence we owe.

A Seaside Sonnet

Her heaving roar dulls out all other sounds
Wind a constant swelling curtain, web-thin
That catches threads in hair and hands, around
Fingers, a deafening caress within
Ears. Bodies fight to keep their heat, but cold
Wins at the edges, nerves aching while tears
Of vapor linger, drops of whispers told
By mist and foam of longing, birthed with fear,
Carried deep in hearts dreaming of escape.
Bare feet tread in tidal violences
Where lunar force inflicts every wave's fate
Torn from land in distorted distances:
    Alien and strange this lethal saline
    Beauty in her strength, her serene blue-green.

Duet

Written at Glass Beach, California

On pleasant days she calls to me
Rest yourself, my love, my friend
gently, sweetly
let your roots sink in
her roar a quiet thing
forever spend your days
yet swiftly she will change
watered by my waves
her moods mercurial
endless as the skies
and crush what she'd embrace.
and lovely as your sighs.

Falla(sea)

We never talk about how glaring is the sea,
a vast wilderness without shade, without mercy
a type of desert, only suited to the natives
and we, trespassers and foreigners, blindly invade
the sun piercing our eyes as we try
to swallow the colors and the light
summer's promise of wind, waves, respite.

Gray Veiled Afternoon

Written at Pudding Creek Beach, California

Two lone walkers pass each other in broad circles.
The sun's glare swells the fog, turns bluffs and trees into phantoms.
Unseen *Panthera* roar eternal, swish paws and tails in vapor grass.
The chill wind breathes, teases wisps of glitter-veined spray.

The mist grows bright with sunlight, blinds the walkers in a silver haze.
They pace one end to the other, feet bared to greet the waves
that rush to meet them, old friends long separated.
Wet sand caves to their intensity; skin soaks the cold into every foot bone.

The surf bounds away and back, jumps to pull at pant legs.
The fog sails restless over inlets and trellises and lines of jellyfish,
the worn road wrapped in shadows like a cloak.
Nothing exists but light and water and lions.

Ocean Pops

In the American "Pops" Haiku style as explored by Jack Kerouac

The ocean's words
Catch on trees –
Wind a thief

Sea winds
Cancel noise
Inside

Breakers
Batter sand:
A soothing violence

Tree trunks
Swallowed by waves:
Feet sunk into sand

I Will Await You

Time dances his way
Into eternity
Captive and free
Endless stream to ocean,

You and the Light
Keep changing
Running paths
I can't see,

I and Breathing
Both still and rushing
Eat sight, scent, sound
Rip apart to feed,

Time, both hero
And villain,
Hurries along your race
Prods at my lungs,

Light and Breath
What we left
When we've ended
And joined the sea.

Premeditated

Winter-frozen flagstone
Reminds my feet of the ocean's cold
Waves rushing over sand
Ever stretching her hands
Further inland

Like the mysteries she holds
In her depths
Aren't enough – she
Must have them all

Leave nothing for the forests
And mountains
The whole planet united
Under her strong arm,

Perhaps an act of rage
Revenge against the bounds
Placed on her: she yet remembers
When the universe
Was only light and dark waters
Perfectly content that God should stop there

But now confined to only reach
The point of highest tide
White satellite her ball and chain
Clouds the gathering of her angst
And ire, rain her grief
That grants life to lung-breathers –

Without her, the world were desert
Killed by relentless sunlight,

Like we're killing it
With Industry's ceaseless refuse.

The Earth lies still, impatient
Plants on our windowsills
The first wave
Waiting for word to shed
Their slow-growing tissues
And strangle us in our beds

Feast on our bodies' cells
Drink the ocean's tears
No longer of hate but relief
Cities crumbled to rust
Planet finally free
Of this parasite "humanity."

What traitors my feet are
To long for she who
Given the chance
Would drown me
Return my bones to mud
Erase my existence
From history's pages

One down, billions to go.

The Curious Octopus

For Shawn Gorritz

1
Shy eyes
Dart, hide, peer up
At me
From coral bones
One arm curling.

2
With eight long arms quite nimble
No bigger than a thimble
Strong as a crab
It glomps and grabs
My slow, clumsy fingertips
Mighty suckers pinching skin

Blooming Detritus

Inspired by "Once Upon a Sea" by Wenqing Yan of Yuumei Art

What magic has she
To make flowers grow
Right there on the beach?
From the palms of her hands
They spring, blooms neon blue
Unnatural leaves and shimmering seeds
Greener than the grass
Of manicured landscapes,

Effortless she sleeps
Perhaps dreams them to life
Crowned about her hair
Her heart
Rooting her to sand
A creature half of land and half of sea.

The surf curls its claim
A grumbling madness
Grasping ever up, ever in
White bones tossed in restless waves
Iridescent sheen glittering between
Jagged glass pounded smooth
Blinding glare of synthetic tubes,
Brightly colored caps roll and clack
Through rings of plastic –

Evidence of humanity's audacity
Slow strangling worlds we've never seen
Murder and neglect
Prices of convenience, progress
Socially conditioned
To never care, or even ask
If the ocean creatures scream.

The Sea Witch's Daughter: A Ghost Story

Seething wet her hair cascades
drenched in angry lashing rain
gown as pale as frothing waves
tangled severely around her legs.

Soaring high on wings bone white
alabaster raven captures light
from fullest icy moon, sunshine bright
glaring visage against the night.

Clouds split like stone lightning struck
Waves of the deep howl and buck
setting sailors' blood to roil
as they cling to reassuring soil.

Oft the cliffs she's seen to climb
arrayed in ghostly veil, high
on bluff peaks she wandering strays
shadows dance her limbs like stains.

It's said that she in roaring squall
lost her lover to the sea, but with all
such tales barely the truth remains: she
looks not for false love fled, nor seeks

any soul in water drowned – the sea witch
from land her heart bewitched
in revenge for love turned faithless:
for sweet lips and warm caress

a mother's loyalty exchanged. Enraged, she
cast into brine the tender thief
transformed, air never to breathe,
and cursed bride to die if she touch the sea,

forever fated the tides to chase
grief burning in her eyes and face.
Alas, one night she screaming plunged
from headland edge to her captive love

that in death united they might be –
but the sea witch's spell merciless reached
to chain her soul to dirt and stone,
and at fullest moon her wails still chilling echo.

Reunion

The ocean is gentle today
benignly chasing children and dogs and gulls
trailing after me like a bride's train
sometimes tangling about my legs.

She seems so sad with haze
clinging to her blue, horizon obscured
by smoke signals from fires further north
the sea helpless to give aid.

She shows her age
in tarnished silver-brown
like a wizened grandma to a child
suddenly ancient, wrinkled and small.

It's been so long since I last reached her
felt her cold hands on my skin –
my feet draw me closer to curling surf,
seek to fail at playing tag

like a tiny child delighted in the catching
the joyful hugs and kisses
and wriggling her escape in giggles and shrieks
stumbles off again, ever looking back.

Tidal matron arms wrap around my knees
reacquainting us with our familiality;
a knot somewhere inside finally releases,
roots deeply drink,

my washed-out footprints
a melancholy song of how long I stayed away,
how long I'll stay away again,
her little desert-dwelling ocean girl.

Originally published in Trouvaille Review, 2021
Re-published in the poet's collection *The World Eats Love*, Ravens Quoth Press, 2023

Welcome Home

She longs to know the sea
its tempers, its seasons:
warm sun singing
on playful surf,
or icy hail stinging
siren tails
gray and crashing
angered to despair;

soft caress or freezing gale
let her always feel
the roar of folding waves,
the constant hiss of wind,
what climbs into curled shells
to hide and live there.

How many moods has the sea?
how many metaphors for its sounds?

Hymn of the deep, a cello
weaving smoothing scores
amid the seagull's squall
the crow's caw
the seal's bark
the shudder of a rolling barge,

the rustle of its waves
a thunderclap
or a shush
crashing a million times on sandy shores
breaking its breakers into shards
glistening skyward off pitted cliffs.

A thousand words fail
to express the majesty of the sea
and the incomparable
"welcome home"
washing over her feet.

Coastline

Written in Albion, Mendocino, and Fort Bragg, California

Land of barren driftwood trees,
glittering baubles hang from lowest beams
of flat-topped evergreens;
over foaming surf and jagged cliffs
roseate petals drift
decorate the ocean breeze
ballet with light and leaves.

Breached into the wide Pacific
rocky bluffs a fortress stands
against the rising tide –
windswept headlands
crowned by mist and wildflowers
stretch in vain pale-barked arms
to pierce a cloudless sky.

I would that I could steep my skin
with the sea's saline scent,
or its gentle thunder bottle
and carry back with me
to arid lands
where its song can never reach,

remember forever the sight
of rocky palisades
glowing red with hazy fire
lined by shores of blackened sand
plunging through the endless deep:

void bespeckled with glittering stars
cradled in the hands of God.

Slow Breaking

She stands long in the water, shrouded in fog
the sun a lamp bulb
clouds and mist its shade.

Long she stands, pant legs
at her knees
waves rolling, running
rushing to her, away.

Cold they splash, crash
surf obscured by gray. Cold the air
and heavy, dripping
from her coat, her hair.

The waves rumble, roar, long they
grumble,
trundle over shore
shell debris tripping their shuffling feet.

Long I watch her from behind, Time
a suspended vapor,
her steps coaxed further in
further in
and when the sun sinks into the sea
she'll disappear without a trace
nothing on shore to ground her feet

and long on the cliffs I'll stand,
watching the breakers roll and foam,
my soul therein
stolen from me
so I can never leave again.

Siren Unleashed

Something changed
between then and today,

Her chatoyant blue
and lingering fingertips
belie a wild need –
the urgency scares you,

One small touch so mild and tame
then all at once she rushes
grasping
restraint entirely flung away.

She calls to you as she ever did –
beauty and power and soothing rest –
you could drown in her embrace
and there bury
your face and hands and lips

flesh and blood consumed.

Her caress sinks under your skin
lure and hook –
pinprick hole in a dam
longing punches through
devastation in its wake,

You fall into her song,
eyes hypnotized
by what she's been to you
and how at last she desires
your heart and soul

and body –

finally,
just you.

Forgetting Blues

blue
blue as the sea with its heave
and crash, blue as the sky
it reflects back
blue like the landless deeps
that darkest secrets keep,

blue as glacier ice
mirror bright in sun's light
blue like the coral's birthright
swells to reach
streaked clouds in flight,

blue as the blinding flash
cracks the night
icing splintered veins,
blue as distant suns
blazing trails in frozen wastes,

blue like the mourning song
she sings after you're gone
heart bleeding
memories receding
holding hope
only for so long

darkness creeping to spring
as the last fume of light retreats.

Eduard Schmidt-Zorner is a translator and writer of poetry, haibun, haiku, and short stories. He writes in four languages: English, French, Spanish, and German and holds workshops on Japanese and Chinese style poetry and prose and experimental poetry. He is a member of four writer groups in Ireland and has lived in County Kerry, Ireland, for more than 30 years as a proud Irish citizen, born in Germany.

He is published in over 200 anthologies, literary journals, and broadsheets in USA, UK, Ireland, Australia, Canada, Japan, Sweden, Spain, Italy, Austria, France, Bangladesh, India, Mauritius, Nepal, Pakistan, and Nigeria. He has two published poetry collections: *Home Green Home* (Southern Arizona Press, USA) and *Time For Verses* (by Taj Mahal Review/Cyberwit, India).

He also writes under his penname Eadbhard McGowan.

Netherlands – Waterland

Lowlands' fat loam layers,
flat pastureland with large lakes,
on which white sails flash.
Polarity, two extremes:
land and water,
cut into segments,
a farmhouse in the middle,
before it, infinity,
from the depth of the sea
blows a mystical wind.

The eternal threat of the water,
constant wrestling and conquering.
The blue-grey horizon,
behind the dark and silent polders
with the resting herds.
Lighthouse headlights
grope through the darkness.
Flood and snow-white sand,
dunes by the sea, marram grass,
meadows by the mudflats,
the thick fur of reeds and rushes,
returning fishing boats
to quiet, sleepy towns.

The summer with green heaviness,
when everything becomes ephemeral,
melancholic cheerfulness fills the air,
expression of the joy of life,
and Dutch restraint,
accompanied by the carillon.
Evening bells of the churches
ring out over the twilight canals.
Grote Kerk, *Haarlem*, the tulip city,
a picture of *Frans Hals*.

We indulge in glasses of *Genever*,
herrings, coffee, bread, and butter.

The expanse of the North Sea Canal,
which links to the open sea,
destination of the East Indiaman,
mercantile and nautical power,
paired with austerity.

Narrow houses, patrician fronts
along the peaceful canals
to return to them
after a long journey.
Remnants of seafarers,
hawsers, belaying pins,
green and red lanterns of spherical glass,
so they can resist the breakers.

Locks, the phalanx of steamers,
wind-winged ships.
We cast off the ropes,
the drawbridge opens,
sail proud over water,
which is friend and enemy,
omnipresent,
wrestling of Jacob with the angel:
I will not let you go,
until you bless me.
Both inseparable.

The Dutch, ecstatics of sobriety,
seers of the boundless in the limited,
the mystics of everyday life,
all a *Rembrandt, van Gogh* and *Vermeer,*
comfort and cosiness,
freedom and business.

Casablanca

Sounds from the harbour,
tooting of ships,
warning signals of trailers,
yellow dust raised by their tyres.
The soothing salty sea breeze
blows the dust back into town.
Late Friday afternoon,
sunset over the Atlantic Ocean,
floodlights illuminate the quays,
the bustle ebbs away.

Up *Boulevard des Almohades*
to the old medina,
small alleys full of oranges,
lemons and melons
like gold in the evening sun.
The smell of petrol, car fumes,
of Bougainvillea and Eucalyptus
of roasted nuts
in streets, lined by trees.

Under a green canopy
fresh fish from the nearby sea,
a symphony of spices.
Fish stew in an earthenware *tajine*
with coriander, almond couscous,
monkfish chunks, halibut, and bass.
Cinnamon, turmeric,
garlic, cilantro.

Setting sun over the centre,
white houses, palm trees,
a peaceful evening.
A woman at the blue-white sea,
looks into the vast expanse.

East Friesland

Land at the sea.
An austere region with many faces.
Full of light the short winter days,
where the wind over the *Wadden* sea
has plenty of room to take a breath.

Nordic geese on marshy meadows,
travellers from Siberian tundras.
Farmland formed the landscape,
soft hinterland, salt marshes,
with sundew and cotton grass.

Wind combs the marsh flowers,
over them fly black-headed gulls.
Tranquil evenings by the sea.
Ground fog models the land,
where the wind bends
the marram grass,
and plays with the dunes,
weather and tides
determine the life.

A crab cutter accompanied
with hungry seagulls in tow,
who observe the fishing nets
and get the by-catch,
that is thrown overboard.

The moon lets its influence play
and brings back the sea.
Mudflats up to the horizon.
Quiet, but full of life.
Wild tranquillity.
Nativeness

The Land Between the Seas

Vikings set course, north,
up the West Sea shores
past the *Bay of Tears*,
a testimony of mournful deaths
of fishermen, sailors, and merchants,
their graves for centuries.

They sailed to *Jutland*
for the feast of Midsummer Night,
a night with its blue light.
A blue light, painted
by coastal artists, and loved
by poets,
this mysterious evening light,
called the blue hour, so bright,
a calm, limey summertime
before the storms to grey-black
turn the sky.

A tidal world
of eternal ebb and flow.
The *Wadden* Sea. Salt marshes.
Walking on the seabed
when the water recedes.
Out there is so much NOTHING.
Habitat for algae, snails, and worms.
Sheep graze on the dykes.

The shallow cutters in a race with the tide.
They let them fall dry,
the old practice and tradition
testifying patience and passion.
Then rope winches pull cutters
over the sandbanks
until they swim free again.

The builders of sailing boats,
who caulk the vessels,
pour liquid tar, hot, into the joints
to make the boats seaworthy,
paint the wooden boats sky blue,
the colour blue,
the colour of all Danish cutters.
Crab feast, fish auction,
mackerel, plaice and crabs.
Quickly load ice for the catch.

The ancient trade, seafaring,
links between islands and peninsulas,
countries and shores,
the Vikings' sea voyage up the coast
from *Ringkøbing Fjord* to Ireland
to found *Smørvik*
the Scandinavian Butter Port,
tough Viking sailors
under the protection of the gods
Odin and *Thor*
warmed by the herbal dune snaps,
the *Bjesk*.

Let loud their voices resound,
these people of the sea,
hard and resilient.
Even back did they sing
the hymn
"*Der er et yndigt land*" *
Accompanied by flutes
and horns?
* "There is a lovely country"

Irish Coastal Village

A friendly wave from a man
who works in the fish factory.
They have put three on the spit.
One at the start,
the second in between,
the third at the end,
to keep a distance
as if in quarantine
far away
from the built-up land.

But there is only the smell of seaweed
and the iodine of the sea.
Trawlers lie on the water - three
and a few boats.
On a truck
grow-out mesh bags
and steel rebar racks.

A tractor leads a boat to water,
a fisherman jumps in,
starts the motor
on a cold windy day
at the bay
where the sunrays fall
on the incoming tide.

Fishermen in their yellow jackets
throw out their nets
and seagulls glide over them
to see if something is left
to feed their constant hunger.

The spit has its toes in the Atlantic
and beds prepared for the mussels.
Fishermen, weather-beaten men,
in tune with nature,
with the salty water,
hardworking
like those in Galilee
who brought in the catch
on a stormy day.

Sea Ravens near Fenit

I take the boat along the coast,
visit the habitat of cormorants
on their rugged island,
their fortress-like outpost,
opposite the port of *Fenit,*
where yachts bob on the water
in friendly unison,
dreaming of a sailing holiday -
St. Brendan overlooks the bay.

On the coastline nestle villages,
a settlement protrudes, green fields.
Sounds emerge from homesteads,
hammering, noise of tractors,
cattle raise their heads.
One can see *Bolteens*
and I remember the pint
which I drank there
where opposite a horse
got new shoes at a farrier's.

On the water the sun glistens,
the island in the distance
stretches the head out of the sea.
On top perch the big sea ravens,
obviously sociable birds.
Now and then one of them rises,
dashes down, disappears in the sea,
comes back to the top, dripping,
sometimes with
or without prey in the beak,
holding their wings out in the sun
to dry their dark feathers.

Over the blue-grey sea
an elongated band of clouds.
I approach the cormorant colony,
let the boat drift, without paddle.
The sun sends golden rays,
the wide surface ripples,
where tongues of wind descend.
A spell of calm, makes the water
shine and smooth like a mirror.

The shore out of sight,
land seems far away.
Me, between grey sky
and steel-grey infinity.
Lonely seagulls fly.
A tranquil mood ascends
after the cry of a sea sprite
or was it a mermaid
who sang her song, so light,
so ethereal, so weird?

Fish swarm under the surface,
in a water deep and dark.
I approach the protruding rock.
The cormorants are startled,
make noise in their nests,
warn the rest of the flock.
A lively flapping of wings.
They escape into the air,
swoop, and dive away.

Ocean Rage

The storm, northsea-ish,
shakes up the sheets
of sleeping, now awaking dunes.
The seagulls hide
the sheep take shelter
in groomed marram grass,
or in a corner by the dike.
No one else to see.
Just gray foaming spray.
The lighthouse light extinguishes.
A steel-colored wall remains.
The ocean roars,
and howls through the night and day.
The spring tide comes.
What menacingly surges
against the shore
scatters salt into old wounds.

Nightwalkers

Kenmare bay rests calmly,
repeating waves drench my shoes.
The moon sees his reflection in the water
Is delighted.
You can see his happiness.
He shines unremunerated, out of friendship.
I owe him thanks.
Resting on a round stone I wait for the tide.
I am looking for hardly noticed creatures.
To perceive them one has to be of the sea,
an eye on the receding water
with rolled-up trousers or unclothed.

Are they not sedentary?
On the stones and rocks by day
the *limpets* walk at night.
Residents of the intertidal zone,
neither high waves
nor rain or sun
can cause them harm
due to their adaptability.
You think, they are not *sessile*,
meeting them at daylight at the same spot.
During the night they wander,
as a mermaid suddenly finding legs to run away.
They are all on the move in the night.
Grazing algae lawns.

Eileen Sateriale is a freelance writer living in Massachusetts. During her working career, she worked as an analyst for the Federal Government and retired with a pension. Her poetry has appeared in *The Wonders of Winter* and *The Stars and the Moon in the Evening Sky* anthologies published by Southern Arizona Press, Capsule Stories, Poets are Heroes Magazine, Blue Heron Review, Mused Literary Review, The BeZine, and Flora Fiction. She has had short stories published in *Let Us Not Forget* Anthology, *Forget Me Knots* Anthology and Flora Fiction website. She has had travel articles accepted on We Said Go Travel. To commemorate the 100th Anniversary of the passage of the Nineteenth Amendment, she researched and complied three non-fiction pieces in the *Online Biographical Dictionary of the Woman Suffrage Movement in the United States.* She is presently drafting a memoir that she hopes to share with her children and grandchildren.

Last Supper

Predatory black buzzards
ominously fly
over the still waters
of the Chesapeake Bay.
A rainy autumn morning
has darkened the once
peaceful summer skies.

Old-time watermen
in work boats drop
their crab pots for the
last harvest of the season.
These frightful birds get
the watermen's attention
with their blood curdling caws.

Crabs that are not fit to be
sold are thrown back
into the silver-gray water
where the buzzards
dive devouring their
blood red carcasses.

Seashore Panorama

Azure ripples sparkle
laced by white cream
creeping on caramel sandy shore.
The tall grass dances in a zephyr
cooling nesting areas for piper plovers.
As the tiny shellfish
burrow back into the sand,
avoiding the creeping water
which recedes,
becoming invisible.

On a neon terry cloth carpet,
seagoers in colorful
bathing suits digest
what lies underfoot,
overhead
and on the horizon.
A sun screened bather
picks up a shell,
inches from her beach towel and
sheepishly holds it to her ear
listening for the waves and
admiring the polished interior abode.

While the sun beats down,
overwhelming olfactory and tactile senses,
nature's headset orchestrates
the sound of the waves crescendo.
A pelican plunges
as a seagull dives in ocean's direction,
and a skimmer skims
while white puffy clouds splotch the sky.

A dolphin swims close to shore
breaking the ocean's surface
then gently receding,
barely causing
a ruffle or ripple
darting in and out,
lazily graceful,
ignoring pocket handkerchief
triangular sailboats
that survey the coast.

Ponies of Chincoteague

Wild ponies don't seem to be bothered
by the heavy, persistent heat beating
down on the unbridled, muddy beach of
Chincoteague Island that they know as home.

They stand in shallow water in this remote
pocket of southern Virginia and hope for
a gentle breeze blowing from Atlantic Ocean.

From time to time, they wave their tangled tails
at pesky flies, wishing they'd go elsewhere.
Then they bow their heads and stick out
their tongues to take a drink of water,
soaking their matted, uncombed manes.

Tourists, wearing wide brimmed hats,
light summer clothes and sunscreen,
who can't be deterred by wild horses,
marvel at these untamed creatures
from a safe distance because they
know that they could be dangerous.

The Final Swim Meet

Today's the day of the final swim meet.
Hot as it is, it couldn't be a lovelier day.
Swimmers apply sunscreen so as not to burn.

To win this competition will be an awesome a feat.
Will the star of the team do well as he competes?
The athletes hope to win on this judgment day.
The coaches cheer the team the proper way
as trained judges evaluate stroke and turn.
Victory, everyone works hard to earn!

The winner's smiling face got quite a sunburn.
He'll savor the victory for the rest of the day
and stay inside avoiding the Washington heat.

Dog Beach

Perfect summer beach day;
seventy-five degrees and
not a cloud in the sky,
Two dogs walk along the water;
one brown, one tan.
They are aware of the low tide
and zig-zag along the dry sand,
looking out for each other,
communicating with gentle whelps.

A young girl digs in the sand
near her parents' beach blanket.
Dad is reading the newspaper
and Mom is perusing a book.
The girl contently builds a sand castle
with bright colored beach toys.
She looks to the shoreline and notices
the dogs frolicking in the water.
She says to her mother,
"I want to play with the dogs."
Mom shakes her head,
"Wild dogs can be dirty."

A crab comes out of the water
and scurries on the beach.
The tan dog spies the crab
and runs in its direction.
Both dogs start chasing the crab
as the brown dog furiously barks.
The tan dog grabs the crab in its
mouth and runs along the beach
with the brown dog keeping up.

The dogs run to the family beach blanket
with the mangled crab flying on Dad's
newspaper. Mom and Dad look up,
visibly annoyed at the intrusion.
The girl, startled by the excitement,
runs to the beach blanket and,
in the process, ruins her sandcastle.
"I want to play with the dogs."

water horizon

flying fish
exploding waves
heaven on earth
sprays the sky

black and blue underside
jellyfish skims the surface
float new life
ink and marine

Evening Melancholy I

A painting by Edvard Munch

A cold November in a Norwegian fishing village.
A desolate, dark seascape with
a solitary, battered rowboat at low tide.
A man stoops in the steeped with angst.
Marks on his sad face indicate illness.
Heavy head supported by hand on chin.
Jagged face conforms with weathered rocks.
Bare trees, a beaten snow-covered hill with a
small lonely abode hidden in bushes.
Brown red horizon with monotone clouds
does not signal hopefulness.

'glades

Wild grassy land, murky brown sand, nature so grand, winds blow grass blades,
tall cypress trees, majestic reeds, creatures appease, wildlife craves shade,
'gators can swim, with tiny limbs, flies find it grim, nature's parade,
Florida sun, bucolic fun, heaven's not done, wild Everglades!

Emily Bilman, PhD is a poet-scholar who lives and writes Geneva, Switzerland. Her dissertation, *The Psychodynamics of Poetry: Poetic Virtuality and Oedipal Sublimation in the Poetry of T.S. Eliot and Paul Valéry,* with her poetry translations, was published by Lambert Academic in 2010 and *Modern Ekphrasis* in 2013 by Peter Lang, CH. Her poetry books, *A Woman By A Well* (2015), *Resilience* (2015), *The Threshold of Broken Waters* (2018), *Apperception* (2020), and *The Undertow* (2023) were all published by Troubador, UK. "The Tear-Catcher" won the first prize in depth poetry by *The New York Literary Magazine* and "Pathfinder" won the Polaris Trilogy Contest and will be sent to the moon's south pole on a time capsule by NASA. Poems were published in *Deronda Review, The London Magazine, San Antonio Review, The Wisconsin Review, Expanded Field, Poetics Research, The Blue Nib, Tipton Poetry Journal, North of Oxford Journal, Otherwise Engaged Magazine, Literary Heist, The High Window, Wild Court, Remington Review, Book of Matches, Lothlorien Poetry Journal, Poets Live Anthology 4, OxMag, San Diego Poetry Anthology, Contemporary Poetry 2022, Ballast Journal, Soren Lit, Southern Arizona Press Anthologies, Poetry Salzburg Review.*

She blogs on her website. http://www.emiliebilman.wix.com/emily-bilman

Barrier-Skin

I had dived gearless down
The bathos of the Coral Sea
And swam among coral-atriums.

A mnemonic coral-branch now bleeds my memory.

From the dim anteroom, they had brought in
A bowl of oil to mend my bruises but my blood
Fomented until we beseeched

The vellum-book of hours
To graft the primal zoo-colonies
With chrorophyll, imploring the hours

To eradicate the aragonite gnawing
Upon the primeval coral shells
On the bare bathos of my gearless dive.

Like poison nettle-welts, toxic palythoa
Polyps had blemished my barrier-skin
With clotted blood and urticaria.

The Dunes

Hypnotised, I gazed and gazed
at the sands wrapped by the sea-breeze
moving the northern sea through
the thick window-panes keeping
the alien ills wind out of the barrier-resort.
On the click of the car key, the jade
sea-air spurred me on towards
the huge dunes of the beryl-beach
spreading out like congregate boulders
tumbling down from the hills.
On the sand-heap, there slithered
a juvenile sand-serpent ready to ambush

its predators by burying its body
inside the soft sands stealthily.

On the Isthmus

So, Odysseus stepped onto his ship
And entered Oceanus, the land's fluvial
Mythic girdle. As he crossed their seas
He warred against the giant Cyclops,
Daring to traverse their danger-routes.

Surreptitiously, the sirens threw
Boulders towards him blocking
The straits. Odysseus thwarted
The spectre-sirens who destroyed
The sailors' desire for women
Deceiving men with their dithyrambs.

Fiery Charybdis schemed, spewed
Ogre-swathes of water and swallowed
The stranded ship. Nude, he hung onto a branch.
Six sailors were ceded to strait-rock
Scylla who consumed them all.
So, Odysseus saved his sea-faring ship.

Summer Wind

The seas begin to swell
tides invade the porous rocks
crabs peep out of stones

A juvenile swan
draws concentric circles
on a tidal pool

Summer wind whispers
people run under canopies
rain opens the skies

Hidden behind clouds
the moon dissolves our shadows
dark drop by dark drop

Challenger

The engine dives yet deeper
Into Orpheus' dark subterranean
Trenches along volcanic vents
That spurt out obsidian gas-fumes
Where bacteria swarms thrive like
Colonies of bees within a wild prairie.

In these ice-waters, all sea-creatures
Are liquified but, on a layer above,
Lantern-fish gleam to prey, mate,
And maintain the primaeval breath
Of silence buried in tenebrous
Shadows before matter began

To aggregate and darkness
Was gradually abraded by light.

The Whale-Song

Lest the sea sing the whale's
elegy, the whale's cradle is kept
untarnished. In memory of the stranded

whale, the sculptor shaped the ship's hull
like a whale's torso incurved
with oak branches, polished,

and smoothened with bee-wax.
He incrusted the ship's body
with lucent shells to safeguard

the whale's cradle and the sea's memory.

The Fisherman

At dawn, the Māori fisherman sailed on the southern seas
on his ancestral canoe that he had scraped and oiled for fishing.
As he left the archipelago, he remembered his dream of a single
red rose traversing the ocean safely back to the harbour.
He had been taught by his father to weave and tie the green
flax-nets for fishing. Today, his canoe resembled a cornucopia
filled with eels, blue cods, mackerels, wrasse, shrimps, krill,
and squids. As he poured the fish into the wicker baskets
he purified them with a *hurianga tangaroa,* his ancestral soul-prayer.
Like an *ika,* the fish-god of his ancestors, tattooed upon his arm,
a foam-feathered albatross flew above his canoe, hovering above
the fisherman. Respecting the ration of wise *tapu,* he prayed
and let the albatross feed on a purified portion of squid.
The wind carried the albatross across the sky-loops spread
like swings throughout the sky. The bird rose, descended,
and glided dynamically along large airshafts but, no sooner,
returned to announce broken weather and gales upon the seas.

Oozing with the burnt-orange and yellow tints of the sun, the waters
gradually turned sepia-brown with wind-tipped sediments.
But through the mist and rain, the rolling waves, and howling winds,
the albatross led the lone fisherman towards the northern port.
As the man glimpsed at the flickering gleam of the lighthouse, he realized
the albatross *was* the spirit of his protective ancestor. The bird regained
his sky-loops, leaving the lone fisherman safe on the southern seas.

Denis Murphy was born in 1959 in Cork, Ireland and now resides in Sligo, Ireland. He was a former Travel Consultant and Travel Agency Manager. A major turning point in his life came in 2007 when, at the age of 48, he was diagnosed with Parkinson's Disease. Anyone who suffers from this Disease, or has a family member who does, will know that it brings about drastic changes. It can be very difficult for people with Parkinson's to express their emotions, feelings and their loss of power and independence. All the more need for an outlet to express these emotions. He believes by sharing he can better understand what he is going through. One can get caught up in their own worries and forget that the disease not only affects their own lives, but also that of family, friends, and loved ones. They often feel as frustrated and confused as he does. He is very lucky to have such an understanding wife who has great patience, empathy, and understanding and provides her support, encouragement, inspiration, and love. The main themes of his poems are about coping with Parkinson's Disease, and his relationship with nature, life and with oneself. Poetry helps him appreciate this wonderful gift of life.

His first book *The Frozen Mask*, was published by Southern Arizona Press in March 2023. It is a commentary and collection of poems to help express his emotions and feelings and to help readers understand the challenges one faces when living with a degenerative disease. Not only the physical symptoms, but the mental difficulties and the impact on one's self-confidence, self-esteem and the erosion of independence and freedom, we take for granted until lost. But also, the life changing challenges that inspire hope and a better appreciation for all life, in particular those close to us.

From a Distant Shore

Like waves crashing upon distant shores
A wild winter's wind rages and roars
Leaving debris strewn across rocks and sand
Creating patterns we can not understand
Neither decipher nor read
Rock and stone, pebbles and weed

From ancient and forgotten places they hale
Scattered seashells, sand and shale
Each stone unique, it's colour and sheen
A beautiful reminder of God's creation can be seen
From the treasure chest of Manannan Mac Lír *
Beyond those rugged cliffs so tall and sheer

Perhaps this boulder was once on a mountain range
In a far off land, so different and strange
Or that grain of sand was once on a distant shore
On the other side of the world, long before
Man walked the earth with such arrogance and pride
Under moon and stars and celestial tide

Perhaps it's all that remains of that asteroid
Which roamed far beyond the great void
Came crashing down in fire and flame
Like a fallen god who had no name
Across the sky, like thunder roars
Bringing death and extinction to the dinosaurs.

Or perhaps in Earth's fiery furnace it was cast
In the deepest canyons and caverns so vast
Forged in molten rivers of fire and flame
A violent birth, then scattered over mountain and plain
A lifetime's journey to reach this shore
From Earth's beating heart, her living core.

*Celtic/Irish GOD of the Sea.

A Country Cottage by the Sea

A country cottage by the sea
With a wildflower garden and rockery
A little patch of heaven for you and me
Where we can sit and chat and dream
And there, at the bottom, a giggling stream
Singing a sweet melody as it tumbles along
As we listen to the birds as they sing their song
A symphony of nature caught on the gentle breeze
A sanctuary from the world where we can be at ease
A rest place for the body we can surely find
A balm for the soul and calming the mind.

Keepers of the Light

In angry seas and storms from hell
They have kept travelers safe and well
On battered coast, raging thunder roars
A ring of Light around our rugged shores

Seafarers and sailors, fishermen too
Saved by a beacon of light shining through
Through darkest night and on greyest day
Coastal fog, sea mist and spray

On rugged rocks they stand alone
At ocean's edge in their Towers of stone
Against the tempest and raging waves
They have saved so many souls from watery graves

Raise your glass and make a toast
To the brave Guardians of our coast
To the Keepers of the Light
Who keep us safe throughout the night

A lifetime of bravery and dedication
A life on the edge between rock and ocean
Thank these men and women for their bravery
Keepers of the Light, Sentinels of the Sea.

Power and Respect

On a lonely headland, a windswept beach
Rugged, razor sharp rocks seem to reach
Like giant stone fingers, pointing the way
To the deep, dark ocean, the Wild Atlantic sway
The west wind howls like a demented banshee
While the Sea God's fury is for all to see
Scattering all before, it has no peer
A creature of power, of beauty and fear
As graceful as a woman, often calm and serene
Explodes with fury, like a warrior queen
Demanding our attention, our awe and respect
Changing moods and emotion, when we least expect
Striking terror and fear, in the hearts of mortal men
As the waves crash ashore, again and again
Forces so powerful so strong and so tall
We huddle for shelter behind a stone wall
As nature reminds us of our arrogance and pride
And that we are no match for the wind and tide
And before such awesome beauty and power
We can only bend our heads and cower
This reminder of her power, nature did send
And wait for the Storm God's anger to end.

Seashore

A blustery day for a walk on the strand
The wind whips up clouds of shimmering sand
Stinging the eyes and tossing your hair
While circling seagulls, their cries fill the air

A flurry of little wagtails, bob and weave
In a frantic effort to retrieve
Hunting for little creatures and juicy sand flies
As evening falls, under darkening skies

With the tide fully in, we sit by the seashore
The beauty that surrounds us, impossible to ignore
Watching the seabirds, hover and glide
Playing games of dare with foam and tide

The Sun sinks slowly into the west
A feeling of calmness, healing and rest
Unable to express the pure joy we are feeling
A beautiful Symphony, a Tapestry of healing

Waves crash and tumble, where earth and sea collide
Echoes of the Ocean's heartbeat carried by the tide
Like a distant drum beat, from the deepest Ocean floor
The Rhythmic Dance of Life can be felt on the Seashore.

The Wild Atlantic Way

Music echoes throughout the night
An open doorway, a welcoming light
Crowded pubs where fiddlers play
Until the dawning of a brand-new day
Tin whistle, banjo and pipes combine
Music Drink , Women and Wine
Bodhran beat and friendly folks
Singing songs and telling jokes
What more could a man want or need
Good company and a massif feed
A feast of pints and getting pissed
The faintest promise of being kissed
Oh the craic is mighty by night and by day
As we journey along The Wild Atlantic Way
Sunshine, clouds and summer skies
The sounds of the ocean and the seagulls cries
White horses ride on rolling waves
Against cliff so tall and magnificent caves
Beaches of gold, edged by water so blue
Fields so green, believe me, it's true
But when all is done and said
From the magic of Mizen, to Malin head
And beautiful beaches like Barleycove
Through peaceful towns and villages we drove
The Kingdom of Kerry and magnificent coast
And of their great footballers, they can boast
Over majestic mountains, deep valleys below
Where the mighty Shannon waters flow

From the Treaty city to the city of the Tribes
A land of saints and scholars and scribes
The beauty of Clare and the mighty cliffs of Moher
The Burren and wild Mayo's rugged shore
Castles once mighty now silent and sad
Through the centuries, good times and bad
Crumbling old churches, overgrown graveyards
The haunting music of those old Poets and Bards
On mountain top, the cairn of Queen Maebh
With tombs and tales of warriors so brave
To Sligo's fair lakes and lovely Leitrim
The Wild Atlantic where surfers ride and swim
And beautiful Glencar and it's tumbling waterfall
Just one of the delights on our journey, from Cork to Donegal.
We make our journey through sunshine and rain
Forgetting our sorrows our worries and pain
On our quest for adventure and some fun
Life passes quickly and we only have the one
A pilgrimage of sorts for the restless soul
As the radio plays that old rock n roll
An experience to treasure that's for sure
On the Wild Atlantic Way, a magical tour.

Shades of Silver

Silver light shimmers on waters, dark and deep
Sparkling like tears, where angels softly weep
On silver tipped waves, white horses ride
Dancing on foam at the turn of the tide
Diamonds that sparkle like stars in the night
Flickering and twinkling in late evening light
Shadow and light meet at the verge
On a rocky shore, where Earth and sea merge

Silver and crimson on darkening skies
As evening light fades and slowly dies
Inky dark clouds, silver sky overhead
Metallic grey with a hint of red
Casting long shadows on stony ground
A hushed silence, descends all around
A ghost like world of silver and grey
As the sun retreats at the end of day.

On a rocky beach and rugged shoreline
Where tide and earth embrace and entwine
Shapes and shadows mingle and blend
Our silent prayers and hopes we send
To whatever gods we kneel and pray
In gratitude for another day
As darkness creeps across the bay
In the dying embers of another day.

Andrew McDowell became interested in writing at age 11, and by the time he was 13, he knew he wanted to be a writer. He is the author of the epic fantasy novel *Mystical Greenwood.* He has also written and published short stories, poetry, and creative nonfiction. Andrew studied at St. Mary's College and the University of Maryland, College Park. He is a member of the Maryland Writers' Association. He was diagnosed with Asperger syndrome, an autism spectrum disorder, when he was 14.

Visit andrewmcdowellauthor.com to learn more about him and his writing.

Sea

A realm of the blue
Many more plants and creatures
Below the surface

Rain from the heavens
Flowing water across the land
Water links the realms

Course of the whales
Journeying over oceans
Sea life and new lands

The whale road
Plus more bodies of water
Honored by the Celts

Offerings were made
In deep and sacred wells
Gifts from the fairies

Kingdom of fairies
World for our ancestors
Under the water

Remember the past
Forbearers who came before
Sailing to new lands

The Blue Crab

For any blue crab gone astray
We all share a destination
Our home 'round the Chesapeake Bay

Whether sparkling or in dismay
There is a joint expectation
For any blue crab gone astray

Respect for this place we must pay
Like a ground of consecration
Our home 'round the Chesapeake Bay

So many of us find our way
Wandering is exploration
For any blue crab gone astray

Here part of us shall always stay
At the heart of a great nation
Our home 'round the Chesapeake Bay

Proud Marylanders every day
Remember whilst in migration
For any blue crab gone astray
Our home 'round the Chesapeake Bay

Voyaging Vessels

Anchored they are along the shore,
Both for those arriving and departing,
Crest gliders float across waters,
During which many can enjoy sailing.

Growingly do vessels voyage,
For even facing peril on the sea,
Cast some have to watery tombs,
Hereafter they stimulate mystery.

In history some are renowned,
Just for brief fame or long and useful lives;
Killed, rebuilt, or even haunted,
Long afterward of life their trouble deprives.

Many more ships shall come across,
New innovations in them they equip.
Old and reliable there are some,
Past and present there is many a ship.

Untitled Haiku 1

A leviathan
Largest creature of the deep
Great, kind, and gentle

Untitled Haiku 2

Never-ending blue
As far as the eye can see
Deep, rich, and wondrous

Water

Swamped with emotion
Pouring like heavy raindrops
Get out of your storm

Lost in fog or mist
To the dirt or the heavens
Keep in steadfast faith

Bodies of water
Good to stop along the shore
Release your feelings

At a riverside
Listen to trickling currents
Or falling raindrops

Blue ever so deep
Hath a drink, bath, or a swim
Sooth and cool your heart

Collect some seashells
Be yourself on your journey
Storms shall flow away

Having sunk so deep
From the blackening depths
Rise upward again

Waves splashing on rocks
Ripples on a pond's surface
Watch and let flow on

Joan McNerney's poetry has been included in numerous literary magazines such as *Seven Circle Press*, *Dinner with the Muse*, *Moonlight Dreamers of Yellow Haze*, *Blueline*, and *Halcyon Days*. Four Bright Hills Press Anthologies, several Poppy Road Review Journals, and numerous Kind of A Hurricane Press Publications have accepted her work. She has four Best of the Net nominations and her latest titles are *The Muse in Miniature*, *Love Poems for Michael*, and *At Work*, all available on Amazon.com

Beach

My mind is an ocean
where swimmers, surfers,
sun worshipers cavort.
Long salty hair
held between
their teeth.
Flourishing
wild flowered gowns
...streams of silk
waves of taffeta
splashy lace.
They sail through
my watery face
combing my eyes
whispering in my ears.
Alone, under a pointillist sky.
Gulls flying around me.
Black waters touched by
moon of vague prophecy.

July

This sun is a giant beach ball
and we can play all day.

Waters creep over my feet.
Should I stand shivering
or go swim? Lose my footprint?

Off I run, falling over myself,
a mug of salty cider. This
wave an insecure bed. Seaweed
pillow. Carried by moon to
an abyss.

The floor of my sea mansion is
not tidy. I shall have sponges
for lunch. Ride with seahorses
perhaps.

On the far shore, my lover
smiles, kiss of surf.

SeaScape I

Hearing waves from a distance and
feeling sea breezes brush our faces,
it seemed a century before we
came to the ocean.

So blue and bright to our eyes
its rhythm broke chains of
unremarkable days.

Over cool sand we ran and you picked
three perfect shells which fit
inside each other. Swimming away in
that moving expanse below kiss
of fine spray and splashes.

With clouds cumulus we drifted while
gulls circled the island. Together we
discovered beds of morning glories
climbing soft dunes.

SeaScape II

Let's dive in ocean hiss swish
riding with bluewhales, bluewaves.
Brush of foam and windy ripples
sunbeams chasing quicksilver fish.

Floating through our shining world
fragrant clouds, feathery clouds.
We weave one arm after another
wearing bracelets of salt pearl.

SeaScape III

Should we just dive in?
See how the sun splashes
through waves...red violet blue.

Weaving around this ocean
my legs encircle your waist.
You are so big and wonderful.

Perhaps we can discover some
great canyons where stars
fell one billion years ago.

I see beams of light in
your hands touching their
cool luminosity now.

Dr. Nora V. Marasigan is a Filipino associate professor in the undergraduate and graduate teacher education programs at Batangas State University JPLPC-Malvar. As an educator, she is primarily interested in conducting studies on mathematics and mathematics education which focus on topics essential to educational innovations. She has been invited as a resource speaker in seminars/webinars dealing with Mathematics teaching and learning, test construction, and analyzing research data. She is a mathematics professor and has published research articles on mathematics, mathematics education, and pedagogy in international peer-reviewed journal. She has also published creative works in a multidisciplinary academic publisher and won the Best Poetry and Best Short Story Awards in the Cape Comorin Writers' Festival 2020.

Eternal Tide

Endless waves crash upon the shore,
Their ceaseless rhythm, a timeless score,
With each crest, they paint the sands anew,
Carving memories that forever ensue

The sea, a mirror of the sky above,
Reflects the dreams of roving hearts
With every tide, it carries away,
The worries that burdened us today

Beneath the moon's enchanting light,
The sea whispers secrets in the night,
Its ebb and flow, a soothing balm,
Guiding us through life's eternal calm

Lighthouse of Dreams

A lighthouse stands on a distant cape,
A symbol of dreams and hope's escape,
Its light cuts through the mist and haze,
Guiding lost souls to brighter days.

The beacon calls to those who roam,
Seeking solace and a place called home,
Its steady glow a guiding force,
Navigating life's uncertain course

With each flicker, a whispered plea,
To conquer fear and set spirits free,
The lighthouse stands, a pillar of might,
Illuminating dreams in the darkest night

Lighthouse's Vigil

A sentinel perched upon the rocks,
The lighthouse stands tall and tough,
Guiding lost souls with its radiant locks,
A beacon amidst the lengthy night

Its steadfast glow pierces the dark,
A guardian of mariners, a guiding spark,
Casting light upon treacherous shoals,
Navigating ships to safe harbor goals

Through stormy gales and raging tides,
The lighthouse keeps watch, never hides,
A symbol of hope in the darkest hour,
Guiding vessels with its unwavering right

Seaside Serenade

A bustling seaside town, where life's in full swing,
Where the charm of the sea makes hearts sing.
Cafés line the boardwalk, bustling with delight,
In this coastal wonderland, a vibrant seaside sight

Colorful umbrellas dot the sandy shore,
As laughter echoes, children's spirits soar.
Surfers ride the waves, with grace and skill,
A life near the sea, an adrenaline thrill

Fishermen's boats sway with the ebb and flow,
As seagulls dive, a graceful aerial show.
Fresh catch fills the markets, a feast for the taste,
In this magical realm, where flavors are embraced

Evening strolls under the moon's gentle glow,
As lighthouses guide ships, a beacon to show.
A life with the sea, where dreams take flight,
In this coastal haven, where hopes ignite

Whispers of the Deep

Beyond the sand and sea, where mysteries dwell,
Lies a realm where secrets are gently veiled,
The ocean's depths, a captivating spell,
Whispering tales of love and ships that sailed

Unveiling legends of untold quest,
Where sailors sailed, their hearts abreast,
Uncharted seas, where wonders reside,
In seashells' songs, secrets they confide.

The briny storytellers weave their spell,
With rhymes and rhythms, they gently compel,
Enchanting all who listen with their might,
In harmonies that shimmer through the night.

The lighthouse stands, an ancient sentinel,
Its beam of light cuts through the misty night,
Guiding lost souls, a beacon through the swell,
To shores of solace bathed in moonlight.

Let us unravel these whispers of the deep,
And dive into a world where dreams may creep.
In the depths of enchantment, our spirits entwine,
Exploring the depths where imagination aligns.

Pat Severin, a retired teacher and member of SCBWI, has been writing poetry for many years. Her poems are regularly featured in the online magazines, *The Agape Review*, *The Clay Jar Review*, *Pure in Heart Stories*, and *The Way Back to Ourselves.* She is honored to have contributed to the Southern Arizona Press Anthologies. This is her eighth anthology.

She is also a published contributor to the books, *I Chose You, Rescue Dogs and their Humans* and *Chicken Soup for the Soul: Lessons Learned From My Dog.*

Her personal ministry is sending weekly cards of encouragement to those going through difficult times.

Lost

The stately lighthouse on the shore,
it asks what mysteries are in store
in dark of night, in winds of storm?
No matter weather cold or warm
it's beacon shines to show the path,
with guiding light till aftermath
of hurricane when seas be tossed
preventing wayward sailors lost
from ever reaching hearth and home
and straying to the great unknown.
'Twould be another lost at sea
from being what, statistically,
has happened to so many men
who never made it home again.
For seas are unpredictable,
from calm to the unthinkable,
from fog to waves that toss the sea.
Without it's light, where would we be?
Stand tall, old lighthouse, lead the way.
Guide on, shine on your bright display
for many who'd forever be
without your beacon, lost at sea.

Beyond the Sea

Anticipating high school
a million years ago,
The year was nineteen fifty-nine.
OK, I'm old, I know.

Transitioning from grade school
I was scared to death.
The thought of high school brought such fear,
I couldn't catch my breath.

But like so many teens today
the radio was on,
and when I heard this song, I felt
like I'd been hit head-on!

And for one fleeting moment,
I lost my high school fear.
I heard the singer of the song.
"Incredible" was here!

I wasn't in the phrasing or
the lyrics that I heard.
His voice was captivating;
With that, my spirit stirred.

The singer: Bobby Darin,
the giver of this gift.
His timing was impeccable.
My fear began to shift.

The song Beyond the Sea for me,
Reminds of such a time
when doubting of myself became
my teenage paradigm.

The times I hear that song played now
I think of days gone by
when I was young, was so undone
and Bobby made me sigh.

My Heart's Trustee

That day in May, when first we met,
I wished you'd go away!
I told myself I'd never fall
for that worn-out cliché.
Why is it that so many men
when asked, "What are your likes?"
will say, "Romantic seaside walks."
I hoped for, "Riding bikes,
or live shows, movies, concerts, too,
but walks along the shore?
I was so sure that we would be
one date and nothing more.
That proves that we can never know
the way love comes to be
and why I'm sure I'd never know
who'd be the one for me.
I might have missed this life we have
with that one bad assumption.
If I had acted on that thought...
it might have meant destruction
of what we have today, my love,
this had not developed.
Just looking back, the thought of that
has made these old eyes well up
because I know from that day since
that you're the one for me.
A man who liked those seaside walks
became my heart's trustee.

The Sea

The sea, engaging, beautiful,
deserves respect and love.
She rules the life within her depths
as well as, birds above.

The sun awakens kissing her,
imbuing her with light.
Nocturnal moonlight changes her,
reflects the flickering night.

The sea, much like a woman fair
wields strong, yet gentle might.
That's why when storms and winds abuse,
she'll never yield the fight.

At times she is benevolent,
contributing her treasure.
sustaining those who live within
for it's her greatest pleasure.

Our union is a perfect bond,
The glorious sea and me.
I'm blessed to see the sides of her
that very few can see.

The sea can sense my deepest thoughts
and so in contemplation
the sea and I engage our souls
in quiet meditation.

Explain our symbiotic pull,
impossible for me,
for what we have is mystical
And will forever be!

She Sells Seashells

(Earl & Jane, Brother & Sister, having a shell of a conversation)

Jane:
"Hey, Earl, I met this lovely girl.
She's someone you once knew.
She's got this place, a special space.
Says she remembers you."

Earl:
"Who is she, Jane, what is her name?
I'm busy, make it clear?"

Jane:
"It's fun to guess, a kind of test!"

Earl:
"Your test is very queer
and isn't fun. My guessing done.
Just tell me, what's her name?"

Jane:
"Ok, Ok, you. Be that way!
I guess you don't like games.
She's Sally Sue, she asked 'bout you.
Stop by there, if you can.
She's at the shore, a little store.

Earl:
"But where? The shore is quite a span."

Jane:
"She bought the store from Mr. Moore.
He had that place we'd go
When we'd catch fish, for licorice whips."

Earl:
"…a long, long time ago."

Jane:
"I know, you're right, alright, alright."

Earl (interrupting):
"I know the place you mean.
Let's stop all this, I couldn't miss
that place. Bet it's still green?
"What does she sell, this Sally Sue?
I can't recall her face."

Jane:
"Why, shells, of course, a perfect source
for beauties, quite the place."

Earl:
"Reminds me of that rhyme we loved,
that talks of selling shells?"

Jane:
"Yeah, that's the one, but now I'm done.
That gave me dizzy spells!"

Earl:
"I know. That rhyme in double time…
Could be a real tongue twister.

Jane:
"That's why I say, she sells her shells
To every miss and mister."

Earl:
"Yes, I'll stop by, I'm not sure why.
But I don't know which day."

Jane:
"Well, she'll be thrilled, her place is filled!
I hope you'll find a way."

Dibyasree Nandy began writing in 2020 after completing M.Sc and M.Tech. She has authored poetry and short-story collections as well as full-length fiction. Her book of 200 sonnets is scheduled to be published in 2023. Many of her individual pieces have appeared in 58 anthologies and magazines. Her first work has been enlisted in the *Journal of Commonwealth Literature.* She is from West Bengal, India. She has two books of poetry, *Fireflies Beneath the Misty Moon*, a collection of ekphrastic poems inspired by Japanese art and *April Verses*, both published by Southern Arizona Press. This is her sixth appearance in a Southern Arizona Press poetic anthology.

Brine-land

The rocky lighthouse of days gone by,
Shades of mauve, the gulls cry,
Frothing and splashing,
Against the boulders, the teal waves crashing,
As the dusky veil descends; a pretty sight;
The hamlet swathed in a golden light.
Where the sea drops to the rim of the earth, a tangerine tint,
The village aflame with activity, a boisterous glint,
Supper to be prepared, stone chimneys blowing off smoke,
In the salty wind, many a rippling cloak,
The waters busy too,
Shifting colours, from yellow to peach, grey to blue.
Indigo roofs flanked by fences and hedges,
Floral overgrowths blossoming as wedges,
Magnolia, roses, lilac, lily,
Olive bushes thriving near the far edge of the bourg, hilly.
Never tranquil, the land of brine,
The din of the crests and troughs always accompanying, when folks sleep, when they dine,
A town of Neptune's music, Poseidon's melody,
Cheery are the residents, their lives entwined in harmony.

Colonial Ships from Over the Waters

Fluttering masts, grey and slate of gloom, murk,
The colonial ships arrive at dawn,
Rippling servitude, the pier in the dark,
Old houses by the coast, foreigners scorn.
At the dock; riches, wealth overflowing,
Traders of opulence from beyond seas,
Back aches, the fisherman's stomach growling,
No haul for lunch, the skins of his limbs crease.
The tempestuous breeze from distant lands,
Dimness of the waters mirrored skyward,
Rapid pendulum, frenzied clock of sands,
Blank pages of history penned backward.
The nautical noose of imprisonment,
Naval lords approach to sow discontent.

Where the Gulls Fly

Beside the dunes of sand golden and white;
A frothing, sapphire body; tumultuous; awe-inspiring and reverent, a humbling sight;
The clouds in the horizon so clear;
The many-hued shells gifted, so dear;
Origin of all life underneath the turquoise, aye;
Where the gulls fly.
The emerald crests, the cerulean troughs, the distant indigo, low and high;
As the foaming tides encroach, the silver rays sigh;
Dusk arrives with buckets of paint;
Jade and teal, mauve and pink, magenta and scarlet, orange and yellow; swathed without restraint;
Peach shimmers;
And rose-red glimmers;
Amidst the blues, gentle;
Twilight's crimson mantle.
Traders seeking wealth set sail;
The men on the vessels with cups of ale;
The wind of brine upon their faces, pleasant;
Compasses in the dark following the undulating reflections of the lunar crescent;
Hoping to return with diamonds and rubies from lands far;
Their beacon in the night sea, the pole star.
Cliffs and rocks;
Caves, isles and hillocks;
Manors lonely at the edges of precipices steep;
Where only forsaken witches live as ivies twine and creep.
Boundless, ageless oceans five;
Interspersed by continents seven which perpetually thrive;
The earth's flowing, gossamer gown, Panthalassa;
Now old and ripped; a goddess that bore many a mountain towering over the stretch of Poseidon's feeding grounds, voila!
Surrounded by corals, turtles drift;

Under the glistening surface, a whale swims past an ancient rift;
Rippling shamrock, fluorescent lights, plants of swirling shades;
Hardly any sterling beam from the celestial Empyrean field
pervades.
Sharks and eels;
In their quest for meals;
An eco-system complete, beneath the bay;
Pearls in oysters on display.
An enchantment cast, you might find Aquarius the mermaid here,
not in the Elysium;
Writing runes of eternity… Look, come!
Or Aphrodite and Eros, the bond of Pisces, mother and son;
The marines and the terra firma; together as one.

Sailing

The ship teeters upon the Aegean Bay;
A speck of white amidst sapphire;
For a day calm, the sailors pray.

In sight, not a quay;
Silver rims atop the waves entire;
The ship teeters upon the Aegean Bay.

Early morn in May;
Near the Grecian empire;
For a day calm, the sailors pray.

A frothing and foaming fray;
Hues of the late noon lighting the vessel like fire;
The ship teeters upon the Aegean Bay.

On the deck, waters spray;
Variety of dinner's repertoire;
For a day calm, the sailors pray.

Clouds turning glum and grey;
Sea-scape dire;
The ship teeters upon the Aegean Bay;
For a day calm, the sailors pray.

Amanda Valerie Judd returned to school to earn her AFA in Creative Writing from Normandale Community College after a 25-year career as a paralegal. She is currently attending Southern New Hampshire University for her BFA in Creative Writing - Poetry. In 2020, she won the Patsy Lea Core Prize for Poetry. In 2021, her poem, "My Only Label" was nominated for *Best of the Net 2021*. In 2022, she won the St. Joseph County Library Spill the Ink Poetry Contest (Adult Division). Her work has been published or is forthcoming in *PAN-O-PLY* Magazine, MockingOwl Roost, Trouvaille Review, Prospectus, and Talking Stick 31.

Visit her at www.amandavjudd.com.

Return to Florida

The airport's automated doors slide open
inviting me into paradise;
moist air encompasses me -
a warm, damp blanket;

My brittle Minnesota skin sucks
in the hydration like an ill-mannered child
slurping his soup;

The balmy night welcomes me
like the prodigal son
finally returning to the fold;

Sand beneath me molds
to the contours of my feet,
rising up between my toes,
becoming one with me;

The expensive, fruity drink,
a much-needed tonic to my soul –
its colorful umbrella winking
like an old friend who knows my secrets;

The snap of the crab leg,
slide of the meat, morsel dropping into
my mouth – all moves to a dance my
hand remembers well;

Hot sun caressing my body -
a long-lost lover
rediscovering every inch;

The surf beckoning to me,
again and again, until I submit,
waves whispering the secrets
of the Gods in my ear –
the tiniest of shells
their telegram;

The sea breeze kisses me
as it rushes past,
reminding me of dreams unfulfilled;

A pelican lands on the pier next to me,
and feels like a sign -
Florida is glad to finally have me
back in her arms.

The Mermaid

Hold me near,
listen closely
and you may hear
the sounds of the ocean
in my breath
as it's carried on the sea breeze;

Savor my kiss,
wet and salty
like ocean spray
accompanied by my turbulent heartbeat
thundering like waves
upon the shore;

Grasp my curves –
extreme, violent –
round and round, over and over,
like sex itself
crashing into the spiney reef;

Yield to my touch,
tiny whorls like swirls
in a seashell,
and yet, sandpapery
like thousands of gritty granules
blowing against your skin;

Worshíp my beauty –
unparalleled, unrivaled –
a rich, delicate tapestry,
woven by God
from the colors
of a late summer sunset;

As I depart,
inhale me,
struggling to keep
even the faintest reminder of me . . .

coconut and flowers,
fish and saltwater,
lust and redemption.

Reach the Beach

a blue cotton candy sky
cinnamon skin decorated with pink frosting triangles
mixed with coconut, Coppertone and conch shells
walking on saltwater, high on happiness, drunk on sunshine
all day, from *Here to Eternity* . . . as far as the eye can sea . . .
to the crimson citrus horizon
where it flows over the edge like a waterfall
no worries, no cares as we listen
to the subtle sounds of a thousand waves swirling
in the smallest of shells tossed recklessly upon the black sand

Tranquility

cool to the touch
even with such sultry heat,
cradled in relaxation
upon the smooth sands,
azure blue Heavens
blanket Aegean-colored seas
separated only by the fine line
where sailboats dance on wistful waves
while their sails flirt with the winds,
floating ever-forward
never quite reaching their destination,
a balmy August day
off the coast of Greece,
sculpted perfection in marble
frozen forever
in your hard, cold, icy blue

Victoria Puckering goes by the poetic name of Toria and the Naked Poet. Her work has been described as naked and raw. She lives in Yorkshire, England.

She writes original poetry of all genres and has only been writing for about four years. Her poems have been podcasted in New York, USA and Drystone radio, Yorkshire, England and also various poetry sites on Facebook.

Last year, she became a published Poetess. Her poetry has contributed to the following anthologies:

The Poppy: A Symbol of Remembrance, *The Wonders of Winter*, and *Castles and Courtyards* published by Southern Arizona Press as well as The Dark Poetry Society anthologies and Wheelsong Poetry.

The Earth Met the Sea

The earth met the sea
My feet touched the sand
As I looked at the water
I saw this big beautiful fish bowl
Of colourful
Worn pebbles and stones
The seaweed that lands on this deserted beach
I imagine the coral city that lies deep underneath
The beautiful colours of life that stand out
As the fish and the crabs and octopus swim about
The beautiful curves and colours underneath the deep blue waves
I feel the current of the sea
This Earth forever moving clearly
Changing as the world hits my feet
This giant fishbowl of Earth's
We can touch
Always just within our sights

The Naughty Little Seagull

I just wanted to go to the beach
Have a stroll
I was hungry
I got something to eat
Delicious fish and chips
A sprinkling of salt and vinegar
I started to stroll
I started to eat
Only to find a hungry seagull looking at me
He was looking at my tea
He was looking at me
I ate my chip
He suddenly flew quickly by me
He snatched my delicious tea
He was now no longer hungry
His belly will be fat and full
Delicious fish and chips
A sprinkling of salt and vinegar
The naughty little seagull

The Sea

The rush of the white wash
Covered the pebbled beach
I felt the seaweed and refreshing water
Wash beneath my bare feet
I felt the cold
The beautiful sea
Behold

'ull's Work of Art

A beautiful work of art
Is historical Kingston upon Hull?
It is difficult to know where I should start
It is an amazing scarf made with love and full of Hull's beating wild heart
Different colours, humour, laughter and many tears
As our scarf of many bright colours flows in the Humber, breeze
The River Humber's water ripples out to the North Sea
Maureen Lipman gave us all an Ology
William Wilberforce rid us of slavery
Philip Larkin gave us our poetry
The Housemartins became The Beautiful South
We're not leaving DJ, Norman Cook out
The music and drama scene can stand out on its own two feet
Of course, we are best known
For our fishing industry
Too many ships lost at sea
Never forgotten
Certainly not by me
Hull's Headscarf's Heroes, fought for their Fishermen's bravery
Amy Johnson CBE
Flew halfway around the world
Solo
What happened to her?
We will never know
So 'ull is certainly, a rough diamond
With many hidden shiny gems
Brought to life with a colourful flowing scarf
That just happens to be 'ull's work of art

Laura Helona Moverin is a queer Brisbane based writer and poet. She works with teenagers as a librarian. A love of writing and words is a hazard of the profession. Laura came to Australia from Africa as a child as part of the exodus of the 80's. She has three disabilities that keep life interesting.

Stranded

Grief the stones you laid in my throat
Have marooned my boat high and dry
From here I am stranded but able to see on the horizon
That streak of sea, that shimmer of blue
Is seems imaginary I can hardly believe it true
And I feel sad and bitter
From being so may miles from you
Unable to take you in my arms and let it flow away
I live here on my sand bank
Drawing patterns and gathering fire wood
I am just living my life
As if it doesn't matter
As if there was no river or sea
As if there were only me
Although sometimes I write poems
And I send them out in bottles
Thinking maybe someone will find them
And know I am alive back here
I am waiting for the flood of life to lift me up
And carry me out over the ocean
Then I will not think myself alone
Just another child of flesh and bone

A Fish Wife's Song

Deep and vast those caverns be
That keep the dreamers of the sea
Brother whale and sister seal
Are swimming there with me
The tides move the ocean breaths
And from within your fantasies
You can hear my sweet song
Calling the lost to where they belong
And we will string necklaces from the teeth
Of all those who brought us grief
Those who spread oil on the reef
Oh yes you must learn to see
That it is not empty, this roiling sea
It teams, it brims with changing life
Come swim with me your wise fish wife

On the Ocean Floor

When your heart is aching
When you are breaking open
When no words can sooth your shaking
Lie still at the bottom of the ocean
And listen to the hush of the sea
When you are tired of the clatter of words
When people's expectations seem absurd
Then lie with me curled
In the depth of the sea
And we will be as quiet as can be
Listening to the soft humming of the world
Which is the life that exists despite hope
Which requires no more than breath
Which lets the soul rest
And I will hold making space
For all that is broken and in disgrace
My deepest pain
That speaks to me in whispers
And sometimes yells at me
Why won't you listen
And just let me be

Selkie

I lie in the curl of a shell
Looking up at the eye of the moon
For seven years I stayed on land
Serving the one who caught my hand
Seven tears he drew from me
But he couldn't take my longing for the sea
The beating heart, the breath of salt
The pathways deep down in the kelp
I am returning to my sister seals
In my little boat of rounded pearl
He stands alone on the shore
Calling, Sarah, Sarah come back for more
But I am not the same as before
And that is not my name so I curl
Into my seal skin once again
And wait for memory to make me well

Mel Edden is a British poet who has lived in Maryland for fifteen years. She reads and writes poetry in her spare time. Her work has been published in The Local Raven Review, Maryland Bards Poetry Review 2023 by Local Gems Press and is forthcoming in 50 Give or Take by Vine Leaves Press. Her perfect day would include a blustery walk on a beach followed by a long read with a nice cup of tea.

Worm's Head*

We walked on the dragon's back while he was asleep
having crossed the causeway avoiding the deep

Revealed by the tide, the great tail of the worm
laid down in the ocean so solid and so firm

A city of barnacles and mussels did pass
and so many rocks were trod before grass

O Gower waters, so blue and so clear
home to the seals who bob at the rear

Swooping choughs with their beaks of red
shearwaters and fulmars, ducking their heads

Meanwhile the dragon rests and his head we spy
a slit for his mouth, a cave for his eye

Majestical beast, we'll forever be in awe
that your fire did retire to these rugged Welsh shores.

**Worm's Head is a headland on the Gower Peninsula in Wales, UK, consisting of a rock causeway which joins the small island to the mainland of Rhossili. Local legend states that the Vikings believed the island to be a sleeping dragon.*

Langland Bay Manor

You looked lonely
and out-of-place,
high up on the Swansea hills,
partially obscured
by freshly-painted green beach huts
and rows of trees ever-advancing.

You looked like you had a story to tell
and secrets to share
with your copper-plated spire,
chimneys tall and countless
and brickwork old and intricate -
if only someone would listen.

I will listen, Llan-y-Llan.
I will pay heed to your history.

Tell me of the ironmasters
of Merthyr Tydfil whose vision
you were on the Newton Cliffs.
From what were they retreating?

Tell me of the miners of Aberfan
seeking refuge in your tranquil rooms.
Were they ever able to forget
those cold, coal-stained faces?

Tell me why a ghostly figure
in a dress of flowing blue
blocks the top of your stairs.
Why should no guests pass?

But, who am I kidding?
Bricks do not speak. You cannot
give me the answers I seek
- so much is lost to time.

But I will not cease to ask.
I need to save the stories
of all those souls who,
through the years,
have gazed from your many windows
out across the timeless sea.

Three Cliffs Bay: A Love Poem

1.

As students we rode our bikes on your sands
across the cliffs at Southgate and down.
The beach was as smooth as it is today,
the sun as bright and the waves as inviting.
We left long, curved tracks for the sea to erase,
having scrambled down steep, sandy paths.
That day is one of many I have collected
- a catalogue of happy returns.

2.

Another time we watched daring mountaineers
ascend the slate grey rocks to your steepest peeks,
kitted with coloured helmets, harnessed by hefty
ropes, belays glinting in the afternoon sun. Then,
at the sound of splashing, we turned to observe
chestnut horses trotting downriver to the bay. That
day of magic, your vast expanses and sandy shores
we shared with those climbers and horses alone.

3.

Over the years my steadfast affections have remained,
despite the humdrum that distracts me elsewhere.
Like a teenage crush, I've tacked prints to the wall.
Like a lover, I've explored you hungrily with my lens
- at many angles and in many shades - first on film
and, more recently, in more immediate pixels. Like
an artist, I have painted you, bold strokes on canvas,
rich acrylics reflecting this endless urge to return.

4.

More recently, with friends, I've clambered your cliffs,
retracing your shores with a dog named Rufus, sliding
down dusty dunes, exploring ancient caves, reconnecting
on your sands, our laughter blending with the breeze.
Finally, today, as a family, we cut through the golf course,
scaled rugged Welsh footpaths to your crumbling castle,
delighting in the call of the choughs, awestruck by the
views and the abundance of vibrant yellow whitlow.

5.

Can a meet-cute exist for person and place?
Every time I return, I recall ours. Me at nineteen,
out to roam, turn a corner and there you were
- the most breathtaking views. I became yours.
Wading your waters, I thought: *I have found
my soul place, there is no space so divine.* Today,
to my husband I say: w*hen I am gone bring me home.*
I will finally give something back - ash and sand as one.

Jerri Hardesty lives in the woods of Alabama with husband, Kirk, who is also a poet. They run the nonprofit poetry organization, New Dawn Unlimited, Inc. (NewDawnUnlimited.com). Jerri has had over 500 poems published and has won more than 2000 awards and titles in both written and spoken word poetry.

Tides - Haiku

High tide tumbles in
Erases each day from beach
Slinks back out, digests.

Lighthouse

See me,
Light in the night,
Heed me,
Flashing bright,
Do not throw yourselves
Upon my shore,
The white, bleached bones
Of skeleton ships
Does haunt me so,
I do not wish to see
Your feral faces
Flushed with fear,
Do not draw near,
Tiny clawing creatures,
Stay away from here
And pass by silent, still,
Do not disturb
The song of caressing waves
Lapping kisses
At the hem of my skirt.

Lighthouse was previously published in Pennsylvania Prize Poems 2012

Morning Miracle

I filled the bucket
With carrots and apples
And added it to the other
Items in the small boat.
I rowed out to the island,
And unpacked,
Spreading a quilt
On the beach
As the sun began to flare
On the horizon.
I waited there
In the early dawn light
Until I heard them coming,
Snuffling snorts
And soft whinnies,
The little wild ponies
That live here.
I sat still, silent,
Watching as they discovered
The scattering of fresh produce
Along the waterline.
With my camera set
To make no sound,
I click and click and click and click
Until the battery runs out.

Morning Miracle was previously published in the Mississippi Poetry Journal, Spring 2020

Seascape

Sea oats
Bend in salty wind,
Nod their heads
Up and down
In time
With ocean breeze rhythms.
Sand sprays
In tiny white fountains
From the tips of dunes,
Dances in rising spirals
With the seagulls,
Settles as a blanket of particles,
Dry upon wet,
And molds itself in,
Becoming indistinguishable
Again.
Birds form living constellations,
Constructing and deconstructing
Patterns
Against blue backdrop,
Feathered stars
Whirling and wheeling
As they feed.
Waves froth and churn,
Wild horses charging
In their crashing foam,
Pounding hooves
Of seashells
Sinking imprints
On the shoreline.

Skin baked golden,
Saline dried
With hair loose and wild,
Bare toes
Wiggled into warm beach,
Playing footsie
With nature.

Bill Cushing, known as the "blue collar writer" from his years serving in the Navy and later working on ships before returning to college at 35, lived in several states and the Caribbean. He earned an MFA from Goddard College. He lives in California with his wife and their son. Now retired after 23 years of teaching college English, he continues writing and facilitates a writing workshop for 9 Bridges Writing Community. Bill has two award-winning poetry collections: *A Former Life* (2019 Kops-Fetherling International Award) and *Music Speaks* (2019 San Gabriel Chapbook Prize; 2021 New York City Book Award). Cyberwit released his chapbook . . .*this just in*. . . in 2021, and Southern Arizona Press published a second full collection of poems, *Just a Little Cage of Bone* this past February. Bill is now moving into prose works by revising a personal memoir, assembling a collection of creative non-fiction pieces, and rewriting a remembrance of his late wife's death. His collection of short stories, recently released, is *The Commies Come to Waterton.*

Pelicans

Slowly circling,
the pelican

drops like a stone
into water.

Then climbing the
air, he stops, and

with a single
motion of wings,

glides on the wind.

First published in *A Former Life.*"

Planking the Tango

Working with Harry, a Polish
carpenter with blunt fingers,
I spent my sixteenth summer
redecking the teak
of my father's forty-two footer,
a cutter built after World War II
ended and ended the line
of sailboats built by Owens.
We cut planks so dense
they destroy metal.
Bit by bit and blade by blade,
the acrid smoking steel
fills our nostrils
despite the Southerly
blowing off the Sound
each afternoon.

The wooden tongues are
snuggled securely
into their grooves—
waiting for the black resin
to be spread: tar
so pervasive, so persistent
a presence
that only a monthly
buzz cut could get it
out of my hair,
and although
my father isn't always there
as I would go through
each sweat-soaked day, it is still
the closest I ever felt
to him.

First published in *A Former Life."*

Sailing
for Joseph Conrad

I have always taken
the four a.m. watch:
those three hours before dawn when,
inhaling the moist sweetness
of a new day, we awake
and escape last night's darkness,

leaving technology
to experience
quiet and primitive satisfaction.

The ocean rushing underneath,
its volume
dependent upon current hull speed,
spills a phosphorescent wake —
the only natural source of light
besides the moon.

Rolling up and down,
swaying into balance
on the balls of my feet while
cradling the warmth
of a mug's contents.

Soon
an orange sliver appears
and grows, as the sun
finds the seam in the weld
that fixes sea to sky.

First published in *A Former Life.*"

Rp Verlaine lives in New York City. He has an MFA in creative writing from City College. He taught in New York Public schools for many years. His first volume of poetry - *Damaged by Dames & Drinking* was published in 2017 and another – *Femme Fatales Movie Starlets & Rockers* in 2018. A set of three e-books titled *Lies From The Autobiography vol 1-3* were published from 2018 to 2020. His latest book, *Imagined Indecencies*, was published in February of 2022. He was nominated for a Pushcart Prize in poetry in 2021 and 2022.

Joseph Gelosi is a lifelong newsman, writing and producing network and local news programs in and around New York City since 1986. His poetry has been published in *The Green Shoe Sanctuary* and *The Local Train.*

Same as the Sea

Find me in the dark
with your kisses
and wetness
the rain outside
knows nothing of.

Let us investigate
boundaries the same
as the sea.

We'll go out
further than
It's safe.

Return to sand
each embrace
mocking the chill.

Tell me before
the eavesdropping moon
all you want
from sex
Is to come in waves.

Published by Fiddles and Scribbles (2020)

Lost Sailors of Odysseus

(written in collaboration with Joseph Gelosi)

I steered the ship
away from course
the captain cried
who dares?

The mermaids
laughter still
in my ears

A fool's errand
the ship had sailed
uncharted waters

The Captain fully
mad kept staring
out to sea.

Where Poseidon
awaited us
laughing

In leg irons
my only hope
her voice in my ear.

Lost sailors
of Odysseus
useless all

They strapped me
to the mast/the blood from
the whip was hers.

Forsaken to a raft
I was sure the mermaid
would save me

But loving a mermaid
is like chasing a dragon
spouting fire

softer/more wet
my mermaid
my love

clutching at air
I went under
the waves

Woke up on sand
to hear her
laughter

salt dried lips gasping
for help

but I was alone
again

Written by Rp Verlaine and Joe Gelosi

Blueprints on Beaches

Past in/different;
sever my soul,
see it on fire.
Touch me until
I only feel you.

I am almost new
to disappointment
since we met.
All the wrong directions
behind me now.
Run while I dance,
jump while I fall,
hunt while I hide.
I am listening to
my heart for once.

All of the colors,
familiar patterns of stars,
each snap of a wave.
I'm no longer outside of
looking in your eyes

Best are the footprints
we make in the sand,
the oceans erase
walking in moonlight
we know is ours.

Published in 2020 by rudderlessmarinerpoetry.com

Ken Allan Dronsfield is a disabled veteran and prize-winning poet from New Hampshire, now residing in Oklahoma. He has seven poetry collections to date; *The Cellaring*, *A Taint of Pity*, *Zephyr's Whisper*, *The Cellaring, Second Edition*, *Sonnets and Scribbles*, *Inamorata at Twilight* and his just released book, *Aequilateralis, Aphorisms of the Water-Bourne.* Ken's been nominated four times for the Pushcart Prize and seven times for Best of the Net. He was First Prize Winner for the 2018 *and* 2019, Realistic Poetry International Nature Poetry Contests. He has begun producing Creative Content on his YouTube channel and has had success sharing his poetry with the social media community. Ken loves writing, thunderstorms, music, and spending time with his rescue cats Willa, Yumpy, and Melly.

The Artful Weaving of Whispers

The sea, the sea, take me down to the sea.
Wash me in the gentle foggy morning mists.
Feed me with her abundance of fish and mollusk.
Let me dance along her delicate wave crests.
Floating aloft upon an air of pleasure;
stars drifting down towards the water.
A sandpiper scurries across the shore;
The Great Blue Heron silently floats by.
While honeybees waltz around a rose;
Candlewax slowly drips upon my skin.
As a sea breeze extinguishes the flame
music echoes throughout the seashore.
The sky explodes in an aura of twilight;
People stop and stare at the brilliance.
Wavelets slowly wash upon the beach;
I close my eyes and drift into my dreams.

The evening shadows run from our eyes;
Shed not a tear upon the passing of the day.
Fluffy white clouds billow and float east;
A joyfulness still exists in the rolling dunes.
Hazy crimson lights race the falcons wing
as swallows spiral all about the rainbow sky.
At the Jersey shore where zeppelins once rose;
Deeply as woeful eyes can see, into eternity.
As I slowly drift off into unconsciousness
those old memories of when I was not alone
pour forth in an enchanting new kaleidoscope
with vast imagination and electrified emotions.
I beg to depart and plunge into a limpid sea
becoming lost upon the arid shores, into vastness
a lover without love; beautiful without inner beauty
lost but never alone; a victim of guilty pleasures.
Upon the dark evenings of shadowed desperation
with many ghostly spirits residing along the shore.
Dissected voices cry out to those welcoming ears;
Hush and listen to the artful weaving of whispers.

Previously published in *Aequilateralis, Aphorisms of the Water-Bourne.*

Falling Sakura Blossoms

In spring I watched the Sakura blossoms fall
landing in the waters of the Kushi Ogawa River.
The beauty of the tall Japanese Crane as it fishes
along the edge of the water while Canon Birds
fly from tree to tree chasing moths and flies.
In the wider areas of the river, the Hokkaido
Ducks swim while taking turns sitting on eggs.
As the snow melts, we watch as the beautiful
Red Crowned Cranes dance along the shoreline
squawking and singing to all who will listen.
If you are very quiet and still you might see the
shy Sika Deer foraging near the river at sunset.
In spring I watch the Sakura blossoms fall; and
the beauty of the tall Japanese Crane as it fishes.

Spring on the Beach

(A Villanelle Style Poem)

Wild rambling roses of a pinkish bloom
dance to the winds down by the sea.
Roots grasping deep in the tall sand dune.

Pussy Willows growing in a grandiose plume.
Catbirds cry from tall shimmering trees.
Pheasant strut in their feathered costume.

Spring is now here, so we all assume.
A white seagull soars in the blue sky above me.
Sunshine's bright chasing away winter's gloom.

Nocturnal shadows creep into my room.
I fill my cherished cup with a nice green tea.
Colors fill my mind as twilight now looms.

Essence of lilac, such a lovely perfume.
Soon to be May Day and the wonderful jubilee.
Cleaning the kitchen with a sweep of the broom.

Strong winds blow the sand like a simoom.
I sit on the deck with a glass of Chablis,
lost in thought as my old cat grooms.
The last of the sun's rays do heavenly illume.

Previously published in *Aequilateralis, Aphorisms of the Water-Bourne.*

Emer Cloherty is a retired Science Teacher, who lives in the north-west of Ireland with her husband Denis Murphy. She is a Storyteller, Philosopher, Musician, and Gardener who is greatly influenced by the myths and legends of her native culture. Her main motivation in life has always been to awaken in people the love of nature and the compassion that comes from living in a healthy relationship with the world.

She has previously published her works on her own Facebook page, and some of them to the Facebook page of The Parkinson's Carers and Spouses group.

Shore-leave

I could sit here all day
just admiring the view,
and forget all my chores,
and the things I must do.

I forget all my worries,
let go of all strife,
watching the waves in
the wild dance of life.

But they say that the tide
for no-one will wait,
the sun's in the west and
the time's getting late.

And my soul is refreshed
as I turn from the shore,
and take up my mantel
and my staff once more.

Winter Twilight

It is a cold and eerie beauty;
black and silver
green and grey,
with a melancholy music;
ebb and flow
swirl and sway.
Winter Twilight on a rocky seashore.

It is an echo of my thoughts;
turmoil and cares
sorrows and fears.
It is a lancing of my heart;
leaching my pain,
shedding my tears.
Winter Twilight on a rocky seashore.

It is a sacramental balm;
darkness and light,
water and stone.
It is a slow return to calm;
slowing me down,
calling me home.
Winter Twilight on a rocky seashore.

So I sit.
And I see.
And I let the process flow.
In the dark
I return.
And the truth at last I know.
Winter Twilight on the Eternal Shore.

Manannán mac Lir

When my soul is tempest tossed, floundering in anger and
despair,
When my heart feels empty and I find it hard to care,
When the grey world round me fills with hollow fear,
I journey to the edge to seek sweet Manannán mac Lir.

Although is voice is harsh and loud, and fearsome is his might,
I do not fear to call to him, to tell him of my plight.
I hurl my woes into the waves that crash upon this place.
And sea-spray mingles with the salty tears upon my face.

And Manannán, with power and skill dissolves the sharpest pains,
Builds corals out of tragedy, grinds boulders down to grains,
Strews the shore with polished gems, draws ciphers on the sand,
And teaches time and tide lore to his children on the land.

So come with me and listen to the master of the deep.
His songs will be your lullabies and bring you healing sleep.
Eternal tides will energise the heartbeat of you days.
His wisdom will unfold the path through sorrow's tangled maze.

Karen A. VandenBos was born on a warm July morn in Kalamazoo, Michigan. She has a PhD in Holistic Health where a course in shamanism taught her to travel between two worlds. She can be found unleashing her imagination in two online writing groups and her writing has been published in *Lothlorien Poetry Journal*, *Blue Heron Review*, *The Rye Whiskey Review*, *One Art: a journal of poetry*, *Anti-Heroin Chic*, *The Ekphrastic Review*, *Southern Arizona Press,* and others.

As Softly as a Prayer

I look out the window at the troubled
waves and feel a knot forming in my gut.
Low scudding clouds cling to the shoreline
as if trying to anchor themselves against
the fast approaching storm.
I grab my tattered blue raincoat and find
my way to the lighthouse, its beacon
fading against the fury of the sea.
In the cove, the small fishing boats bob
up and down as if saying yes to what they
know lies ahead.
I hug myself and think back to yesterday
feeling the pull of a thousand threads of
memories wind through me.
When the wind suddenly shifts and screams
like a lost soul crying for its mother, I know
why he kissed me as softly as a prayer.

Blow Me Safely Home

(a sea shanty)

It was off the coast of Ireland
when the top sail caught the gale,
and Callie Jo knew she must steer the ship
away from the gut of the whale.

She glanced to the north and there she did see
a cloud coming at her as big as a tree.
She hoisted the main sail and stared into the wind
and took more than one sip of her tonic and gin.

(chorus)
Blow ye winds in the morning
Blow me safely home.
Let the waves rock me gently
Wherever my ship shall roam.

She sang the songs of mermaids,
the ancient mariners taught her well.
She saw the warning in the red of the sky
and knew she'd have another tale to tell.

She lassoed the lightning and cursed the sea
and cast her prayers far and wide.
Soon the stars twinkled and the waters stilled
and Callie Jo silently followed the tides.

(chorus)
Blow ye winds in the morning
Blow me safely home.
Let the waves rock me gently
Wherever my ship shall roam.

Sands of Time

Born a child of Pisces she is taught to
follow the river, to dip her oars deeply
into the still waters and retrieve her
history from the mouths of minnows.

The grandmothers teach her to read
the ebb and flow of the tides and to
know her emotions by the rise and
fall of the waves.

She listens carefully as the frogs croak
their nightly songs and to the reply of
the mermaids as they flap their tails
and ripple the ribbon of the moon until
it breaks upon the shore.

Gathering shells she learns to decipher
the language of the whales and translate
the teachings of the ancient mariners who
held the secrets of Atlantis in their sails.

Free to wander across the sands of time
she calls upon the water horse with its
thundering hooves to save her from the sun.
When weary she calls upon the rain and
sheds her selkie skin.

On nights when she is afraid, she swims
with the turtles to the moon then sits by
the edge of the river to sing the stars home.

Mary Anne U. Quibal is a Filipino 4th-year student taking a Bachelor of Secondary Education major in English at the Batangas State University The National Engineering University JPLPC-Malvar Campus. As a future English teacher, she is fond of reading literary works. She believes that reading will enable every person to perceive beyond the horizon and understand human aspirations. As part of her love of literature, she became part of the research with regard to Queer Literature, which aims to promote gender diversity consciousness in a classroom context. Aside from that, she is also an aspiring writer whose dream is to become a published author.

An Old Man

One night with an old man
Awed by waves of sea
Bringing hopes and dreams

He once told me,
Go and chase your dreams
And hold your piece of art against the waves.

But the waves get stronger,
Old man was blown away by the wind.

And father told me: Go and chase your dreams.
Hold your piece of art against the waves.

One night,
Awed by waves of sea
Bringing tears and grief

At the Seaside

Enticed by the burning sky
Looking at the horizon
With hope.

I close my eyes as I feel the rhythm of the waves.
I close my eyes as I hear the wind whisper.
Driven by promises —
Sensing every beat of his heart

A grain of sand pours its last piece.
Deep pits prevailed.
He is walking faraway,
To a place where distance could not reach

Dissuaded by the overcast sky
Looking at the horizon
With tears.

At the seaside where we met
At the seaside where memories are shared
At the seaside where he left me unsung

Sailor

the Sailor continues to Sail
amidst the gray mist.
facing the call of the sea —
facing the uncertainty of horizon

the Sailor continues to Sail
under the cloudy sky,
embracing the gust of the wind.

the Sailor continues to Sail
in the midst of tribulations.
the Sailor continues to Sail
despite the solitariness.

Cynthia Bernard is a woman in her late sixties who is finding her voice as a poet after many years of silence. A long-time classroom teacher and a spiritual mentor, she lives and writes on a hill overlooking the ocean, about 25 miles south of San Francisco. Her work appears in *Multiplicity Magazine, Heimat Review, The Beatnik Cowboy, The Journal of Radical Wonder, Medusa's Kitchen, Passager, Persimmon Tree, Verse-Virtual,* and elsewhere.

A'sailin'

T'would seem quite true I never was
the captain of this ship,
though in my youth I did believe
in charting my own trip.

But Master Time has made it clear
how lowly is my rank.
I've silver locks and aching limbs
and soon I'll walk the plank.

One thing I've learned as days go by
a'sailin' life's rough seas:
It doesn't work to push against
what comes upon the breeze.

For when I tried to turn the tide,
instead, the tide turned me;
the Sea of Life dictates for us
in ways we can't foresee.

'T'is true that we are powerless
to stop waves high and low,
but we can choose to welcome both
the pleasure and the woe.

And so, this ship does carry me
through seas both sweet and tart.
When I embrace my life, I live
with full, contented heart.

Previous published in *Heimat Review*.

Catherine A. MacKenzie's writings are found in numerous print and online publications. She writes all genres but invariably veers toward the dark—so much so her late mother once asked, "Can't you write anything happy?" (She can!)

She published her first novel, *Wolves Don't Knock,* in 2018, and *Mister Wolfe (*the darkly dark second) in 2020. Two volumes of grief poetry commemorate her late son Matthew: *My Heart Is Broken* and *Broken Hearts Can't Always Be Fixed.* She has also published other books of poetry and short story compilations, all available on Amazon or from her.

Cathy divides her time between West Porters Lake and Halifax, Nova Scotia, Canada.

She can be followed at http://writingwicket.wordpress.com

Waves of Madness

We bare our breasts before diving into the depths. In the dark it's warm yet we are chilled. It's the plunge that does it. The suddenness takes our breath until the cold overtakes and numbs us and we think we're warm.

We spread our arms and embrace vast waters as if flying through layers of billowing silk on a hot summer's day. Or maybe it's our bodies unwrapping from layers of inhibitions and shame, floundering through waves fierce and loud.

There's no life preserver. Our choices are limited and we think we're drowning—may even want to drown to avoid suffocation in seaweed.

We see sharks as we move, forcing ourselves to stretch our arms and kick our legs. We hold our breath without swallowing, and when we drink it in we spit it out so we don't choke.

We swim another lap and another and another while embracing tides tamed in our hearts, thankful we took the plunge because it was all we could do other than die and disappear.

We wanted to live and keep ourselves safe before waves covered us forever...

These waves of madness reach for us all in the end.

Previously published in *Water's Edge*, Evergreen Writers Group, 2020 and in *Poetica #5*, Clarendon House Publications, April 2022.

Rhian Elizabeth was born in 1988 in the Rhondda Valley, South Wales, and now lives in Cardiff. Her debut novel, *Six Pounds Eight Ounces*, was published in 2014 by Seren Books, and her poetry collection, *the last polar bear on earth,* was published in 2018 by Parthian Books. Her prose and poetry have been listed in various competitions and prizes and appeared in many magazines and anthologies, as well as being featured on Radio 4's PM programme. She was named by the Welsh agenda as one of Wales' Rising Stars - one of 30 people working to make Wales better over the next 30 years. She is a Hay Festival Writer at Work and Writer in Residence at the Coracle International Literary Festival in Tranås, Sweden. Her next poetry collection, girls etc, will be published by Broken Sleep Books in 2024.

rescue

you write your name in the sand with your finger
so that the aeroplanes up above can see it.
they are going where the sea is Disney blue

but you are down here,
and the sea is brown as biscuits.

you wave your arms in the air like a windmill
so that the aeroplane up above can see you.
it's a bird up where the sky is Disney blue

look my name's Rhian,
i'm down here please take me with you.

Scott Thomas Outlar is originally from Atlanta, Georgia. He now lives and writes in Frederick, Maryland. He is the author of seven books, and his work has been nominated multiple times for both the Pushcart Prize and Best of the Net. He guest-edited the *Hope Anthology of Poetry* from CultureCult Press as well as the 2019, 2020, 2021, and 2022 Western Voices editions of Setu Mag. He has been a weekly contributor at Dissident Voice for the past eight years. Selections of his poetry have been translated into Afrikaans, Albanian, Azerbaijani, Bengali, Cherokee, Dutch, French, Hindi, Italian, Kurdish, Malayalam, Persian, Serbian, and Spanish. More about Outlar's work can be found at 17Numa.com.

Of Sand and Sugar

delicate and deliberate

soft

these spells take time

the last granule
of sugar

its texture scratching
your tongue
my tongue

our tongues are melting

one more grain
of sand

its hour
passing
overturning

history is repeating

Image by Dimitris Vetsikas from Pixabay

Ram Krishna Singh, also known as R.K.Singh, has been writing for over four decades now . Born (31 December 1950), brought up and educated in Varanasi, he has been professionally concerned with teaching and research in the areas of English language teaching, especially for Science and Technology, and Indian English Poetry practices. Until the end of 2015, Professor of English (HAG) at IIT-ISM in Dhanbad, Dr Singh has published 56 books, including poetry collections *Tainted With Prayers/Contaminado con oraciones* (English/Spanish, 2019), *Silencio: Blanca desconfianza: Silence: White distrust* (Kindle, Spanish/English, 2021), *A Lone Sparrow* (English/Arabic, e-book, 2021), *Against the Waves: Selected Poems* (2021), *Changing Seasons: Selected Tanka and Haiku* (English/Arabic, e-book, 2021), *白濁: SILENCE: A WHITE DISTRUST* (English/Japanese, Kindle Edition/Paperback, 2022), *SHE: Haiku Celebrating Woman That Makes Man Complete* (e-book, 2022), *Drifty Silence* (e-book, 2023), and *Poems and Micropoems* (Southern Arizona Press, 2023, available on https://www.amazon.com/Poems-Micropoems-Ram-Krishna-Singh/dp/1960038087). The poet's poems also appear in the anthology *Love Letters in Poetic Verse* (ed. Paul Gilliland, 2023). His haiku and tanka have been internationally read, appreciated, and translated into over 30 languages.

More at:
https://pennyspoetry.wikia.com/wiki/R.K._Singh
email: profrksingh@gmail.com

At Sea: A Tanka Sequence

the sea smells
from far off leaps to the sky
I drive through
the maze of returning folks
with fresh catch on their heads

watching the waves
with him she makes an angle
in contemplation:
green weed and white foam break
on the beach with falling mood

crazy these people
don't know how to go
down with the swirl and
up with the whirl but
play in the raging water

they couldn't hide the moon
in water or boat but now
fish moonlight from sky:
I watch their wisdom and smile
why I lent my rod and bait

seashore:
she lies on her back
eyes closed
feels foam on the waves
butterflies too

before the foamy
water could sting her vulva
a jellyfish passed
through the crotch making her shy-
the sea whispered a new song

a cloud-eagle
curves to the haze
in the west
skimming the sail
on soundless sea

awaiting the wave
that'll wash away empty hours
and endless longing
in this dead silence at sea
I pull down chunks of sky

a tidal wave
touches the shore to wipe
my naked footprints
and leaves behind some shells
pebbles and memories

Anil Kumar Panda was born in a small town, Brajrajnagar, in Odisha, India in 1962 . He has worked in coal mine sector and writes poems and stories when he gets time. He has already published two books of poems, *Fragrance of Love* and *Melody of Love.* He is working on his third book now. His poems have been published in many national and international anthologies. He loves to write romantic poems and on nature. He likes travelling and meeting people of different nationalities and cultures. He takes inspiration from simple life of the villagers and nature's beauty still thriving in rural areas.

Sitting on the Sands

Sitting on the sands
I watch the sun rising
On the other side of the sea
The blue water turns
Into flames and the slipping
Tides suddenly burn before me

Sitting on the sands
I think about my friends
And foes who love and hate
Me with their moods
I never mind and enjoy my
Moments thinking it is in my fate

Sitting on the sands
I think someday the flame
Will take me as its dear friend
When my moments
Will be done and no one
Will be there to give me his hand

Nancy Julien Kopp started writing in her mid-fifties, fulfilling a life-long desire. Her writing reflects her growing-up years in Chicago and many more years of living in Manhattan in the Flint Hills of Kansas, where she still resides. She lives with her retired husband, is mother to two and grandmother of four. Nancy's stories, articles, essays, award-winning children's stories, and poetry have been published in magazines, newspapers, online, and in many anthologies, including twenty-four *Chicken Soup for the Soul* books. Nancy is a voracious reader and loves to play Bridge.

The Hourglass

Sand collected in an hourglass,
each grain a momentous moment
in years of living, laughing, loving,
as we watch the pages of our lives
turn, one by one, then save.

Piled up in the bottom of the
hourglass, visited on occasion
but never truly replayed,
only saved for posterity,
who might totally disregard it.

Gone is the life that sifted
and slipped through fingers,
young, then wrinkled and dry,
forlorn and forgotten
as the end draws near.

The glass breaks, sending
the sand adrift on winds
heading out to sea, where
the bits of sand and life
join others already resting
peacefully on the bottom.

Raza Ali has roots in Bangladesh and Pakistan, and was born and grew up in what was formerly East Pakistan. He is also partly Iranian and Chinese, and he has come to accept and appreciate hybridity and the fluidity of identity. Raza studied English at Dhaka University and later at Syracuse University where he studied creative writing with the poet Philip Booth and eventually wrote his Ph.D. dissertation on the satiric element in Shakespeare's tragedies. After moving to Toronto in 1974, he worked in different careers but found his most rewarding role in teaching and mentoring newcomers to Canada. Raza's writing, which has included short stories, memoirs, book reviews, and poetry, has appeared in a number of South Asian publications. He has co-authored a book about his involvement with English language theatre in Dhaka, *Curtain Call: English Language Plays in Dhaka 1950-1970.*

Clifton Beach, Karachi

I feel the sand, wet, warm,
in the darkness, feel the sea's
rhythmic breath and his,
next to me
I hear the wave out there
sharing with me its surge of sudden power
I hold my breath as it strains,
hangs taut,
shatters in spent release

I strike a match;
it goes out.
I reach out to him with blind fingers
that he does not feel.

The wave shares with me its passion.
Never dying, never the same, doomed
but finding expression.

He lights my cigarette.
His hands, I see, are not trembling.

The moon might have
drawn us together
down to the sea's verge;
naked, like children
to laugh and splash each other
and submit to the wave's sudden surge.
If only the moon were up
I might have shared with him the sea.

Image by Justie Shea from Pixabay

Jezreel Madsa is a husband and a father of one. He is an English Major, a Blogger, a poet, and the author of *The Greatest Message Ever.* He is also one of the administrators of The Reformed Bunch forum and the former President of Ecumenical Student Organization at Talisay City Cebu. He is also a debater. He has debated several Catholic Faith Defenders online and in public.

He was a former Editor in Chief of *DAN-AG Publication*, a Proofreader of *LIMPID Publication* at Talisay City College. He was also the Vice President of English Aristocrats Club.

His religious orientation is of the Reformed Baptist. His interests are those of the works of the Puritans, Scholastic Philosophy, Presuppositional Apologetics, and Western Literature. He is also a big fan of James Dolezal, Charles Haddon Spurgeon, Francis Turretin, Thomas Goodwin, and Paul David Washer.

Paperboat
(An Allegory)

Heavy were the
sweats and sighs
of the roughest wind
the paperboat paddles
the waves of time

how fair the night watcheth
the ebbs and flows
by mustard faith
the lonely vessel saileth

how astonished the gaze
of the stars that blinketh not;
felt were the jingles of the moon
hushed in silver light

that night that night-- that very night!
alas, the storm cometh in horrendous sight!

row harder and deeper!
plunge it half
ne'er surrender
the canoe of love
the watered layer
kept breaking weaker and poorer

Ocean tears, why us
sinkest and drown?
all of our pieces were
parting us down.

'til the summer days betide
and all the aching waves subside
the wet-papered boat
nay in the blue water float . . .

for SOON in drier land
the hopeful keel will
yonder kiss the ground.

Lariel Manimtim-Mendoza, MAEd, is a 29-year-old Filipina who is married to her husband, Ricky A. Mendoza. She is presently residing at Tumaway, Talisay, Batangas, Philippines, 4220. She currently works as a government/public senior high school teacher at Talisay Senior High School teaching English and research subjects. She is also a guest lecturer at Batangas State University TNEU JPLPC, Malvar Campus. She was a former High School Teacher in San Guillermo Academy in Talisay, Batangas. She loves singing, baking, and cooking. Growing up as someone who's having a hard time to vocally express herself, she usually articulates her feelings through songs, stories, and even poems. She was able to publish her research paper presented in IOER's 2nd World Conference on Education, Law, and Technology dated July 2-4, 2021, entitled *Lexical Semantic Activities and the Writing Proficiency in Practical Research.*

Living by the Sea

Air that is fresher and generally cleaner,
with higher oxygen level, make you sleep even better.
When you'd like to unwind or just want to find rest,
a euphoric mood is set by this soothing sea air.

As serotonin serves as a happiness hormone,
depression and anxiety have no way home.
Up from the skyline down to the sea,
calmness, serenity, and hope you will see.

Troubling skin problems and other health concerns,
once soaked in deep water could give us great wonders!
Physical activities? They have it, great numbered!
Just don't forget your sunscreen so you won't be much
sunburned.

You'll be fitter and healthier than those who lived elsewhere.
In a natural coastal environment, you are definitely stronger!
Feel the nature's healing in your wellbeing and resiliency.
Experience this life when you live by the sea!

Nolo Segundo, pen name of L.j.Carber, 76, became a late in life published poet in his 8th decade in over 155 literary journals and anthologies in America, England, Canada, Romania, Scotland, Hungary, Australia, China, Sweden, Portugal, India, and Turkey. A trade publisher has released three paperback collections: *The Enormity of Existence*; *Of Ether and Earth*; and *Soul Songs* [all available on Amazon]. A retired English/ESL teacher [America, Japan, Taiwan, Cambodia], he has been married 43 years to a smart and beautiful Taiwanese woman.

Ocean City

I saw it then as my own little Shangri-la,
for I was very small and knew nothing
of the big world, the grown-ups' world.

And for the child-me it was nirvana,
that little town on a barrier island
between the gray, cold, untamed and
endless Atlantic Ocean and the quiet,
near somnolent bay where the boats
of the less brave could sail safely….

I could ride my bike from Nana and
Pop-pop's little house on that bay,
feeling as free as the myriad seagulls
swirling forever above my head--
I 'd ride 'cross town to the boardwalk
and if I had a dollar, see a movie by
myself, feeling like a proud little lord--
I remember as though yesterday, and
not 60 some years, my favorite theater,
with its long darkish hall that looked
like the entrance to a pirate's den,
lined with displays of model sailing
ships, mostly men-o-war chasing, yes,
pirates, but never catching them….

But most afternoons I was happy to
just sit quietly on the porch of my
grandparents' house, smelling the
dinner Nana was making while I
read of countless dreams in books,
books that captured like a pirate
his prey, and took me round the
world in the finest and fastest
sailing ship of all—imagination!

Ken Gosse prefers writing humorous verse with rhyme and meter in traditional forms. First published in First Literary Review–East in November 2016, he is also in Lothlorien Poetry Journal, Academy of the Heart and Mind, Home Planet News Online, Southern Arizona Press, and others. Raised in the Chicago suburbs, now retired, he and his wife live in Mesa, Arizona, with rescue dogs and cats.

Melvillian Tales of Whales and Fails
(a Fibonacci verse)

Call him Ahab (not Shirley!), a captain most surly in search of a beast who had him for a feast—one taste and in haste, he spit out the waste.
Ishmael would sail on treacherous seas on a friend's empty coffin with greatest unease.
On another voyage there's blood—and death for Billy Budd.
A short stay on Typee, then flee!
He sought a new crew.
Bartleby
preferred
not
to.

Image by Dimitris Vetsikas from Pixabay

Gordon Smith is a retired public school science teacher living in Hot Springs, Arkansas. He and wife Carol are residents at The Atrium, a place dedicated to caring for those who need the daily help of nurses, doctors, and certified nursing assistants to make their lives as meaningful as possible.

Carol is a retired high school journalism teacher. Both are in their 80s. Gordon is pushing 90. Both love to write, and they enter contests from all over, poetry and short story. Gordon has a book in the drawer of the living room table, where it will probably stay.

The Girl and the Seashell

A darling blond three-year-old
Galloped joyfully through gentle waves that
Brushed the shore,
Loving the squishy feel of wet sand between her toes.
Squealing with delight mixed with a bit of fear,
She watched her feet disappear
As the latest breaker eased up her leg,
Covering it with a thousand bubbles,
Seeming to sigh as it retreated
And gathered its forces for another run.
A bit uneasy, she nevertheless stood her ground
As if daring it to return.
She explored a little hollow
Carved out by the tide's repeated onslaught and retreat.
A glistening shell grabbed her attention
As it tumbled and twisted along,
Helpless against the current.
It was a thing of beauty to her young eyes -
All speckled brown on the outside,
Pearly pink and white inside,
Curled toward a hidden chamber.
She picked it up.
Tiny fingers explored its nooks and crannies.
Fascinated by the contrast between rough and smooth,
She probed the inward spiral.
Something made her put the shell to her ear.
Too young to know that doing so would perhaps
Reproduce the ocean's roar,
She was simply letting all of her senses roam,
As curious pixies will do.
Then she tasted its saltiness.
Next her nose sought to learn what it could.

This was a time she probably would remember always
As she strove to sniff out the secrets of the labyrinth
Which she could not fathom by
Sight, sound, touch or taste,
A tiny claw crept out of the depths
To do some exploring of its own.
Gingerly it touched just the tip of her nose -
Not in a threatening way at all.
The sudden mutual discovery was too much for both:
The tiny hermit crab hastily withdrew its probe;
The tiny tot jerked back her nose, and screeched.
The shell flew through the air
Farther than it had ever traveled
When rolled by restless water - and much faster.

Both bits of life gained important knowledge in that moment.
One learned that some hiding places
May not always be secure.
One learned that the world has mysteries
To reveal to those who are not afraid to explore.
She moved on to another shell.
As did the crab.

John Lusardi lives in Wales, United Kingdom. He is ? years old and has been writing poetry for approximately 15 years. He has had many publications and success in many writing competitions. He usually writes in a free verse style, but also in other forms. He also lived and worked in Southern Arizona in 1998. He lived in Tubac and worked in Nogales.

Horizon "has anybody been there ?"

Look towards that shimmering line of no existence
Is it there ? a goal for swimmers with persistence
White Horses ride and break in its presence
Running shore bound in their effervescence
Fishermen in boats they never arrive there
Although they see it, many fish nets to prepare
In the deep, currents hide beneath its invisibility
Nets cast in its shadow catch fish in all probability
But still it's there a twinkling point in the distance
Unreachable at morning tide, and evenings insistence
Within that evenings flotsam and jetsam glare
Horizon swallows the Sunbeams, although it's not there

Image by Kadi from Pixabay

Tasneem Hossain is a multi-lingual poet from Bangladesh. Her wanderings in other areas of literature include fiction, translation, academic pieces, columns, and op-eds. She writes in English, Bangla, and Urdu. Her writings appear in magazines, different dailies, and annual publications of USA, Canada, Greece, UK, South Africa, China, Indonesia and Bangladesh. To name a few: *International Human Rights Art Festival*, *Southern Arizona Press*, *The Mocking Owl Roost* (USA), *Borderless Journal* (Singapore), *Polis Magazino* (Greece), *Migosepta Global* (Indonesia), *Discover Mississauga and More-eBook* (Canada), *Krishnochura* (UK), *EDAS Chronicle*, *The Dhaka Literature*, *An Ekushey Anthology*, bdnews24.com, *The Daily Star*, *The Business Standard,* and *Asian Age Online* (Bangladesh). Her publications consist of *The Pearl Necklace* and *Floating Feathers* (poetry), and *Split and Splice* (article). She recently published a collection of poetry, *Grass in Green*, with Southern Arizona Press. Apart from the books she has 68 poems and 60 articles published in different magazines of different countries.

She has recently opened an international writer's forum where writers and literature lovers of 20 different countries are participating and exchanging literary, cultural, and traditional views. She also conducts international poetry writing workshop on haiku. Poetry, to her, is music through words; an ever-flowing river reflecting all that surrounds us. She loves to roam around in nature and finds solitude and beauty. Her articles deal with different aspects of life: historical events, interesting facts about different issues and social awareness. Some discuss ways of improving lifestyles and overall well-being of human beings.

She majored in English Language and Literature from Dhaka University. She is the Director of Continuing Education Centre, a human capacity development organization. As a training consultant her expertise lies in Communication Management and Language. She worked as faculty (English Language) in Chittagong University of Engineering and Technology (CUET). She also worked as newscaster, commentary reader, interviewer and radio presenter in radio Bangladesh for 10 years. She has also been active in different sports and participated in some national championships. She resides, sharing time, both in Canada and Bangladesh.

The Lighthouse

Forlorn,
I stand on the rocky mountain, amid the seas and oceans in sight.
Shining bright for the ships, sailing in the dark of night;
Circling, glaring with powerful signs of light.
Illuminating floated buoys, trawlers or ships all alike.

Crystal pearly shiny water and white seagulls.
Nature's beauty to see, for all the sea borne travellers;
Signaling pending doom, throwing flashing lights on treacherous
rocks and waves,
Beckoning humans and sailors, to be safe on stormy bays,
Defying all seasons of the year, ceasing not a single day.

I must go on shining brighter and bright,
When heavenly lights are dimmed by darkness at night,
Fog, thunderstorm or howling seas and bleak weather strikes
I must show them the pathway to their delight.
Guide the sailors home, further away from their plight.

Mostly,
Far away at the horizon I see,
Tumbling feebly the fishermen's boat on the sea.
Coming home, boat laden with fish in glee
Singing tales of forgotten mermaids' plea.

Music playing on the deck as couples sway,
Lovers kissing and maidens stealing their eyes away;
Ships drifting slowly,
Braving death, ferocious winds, whales and sharks.
Till I see only the mast in the dark,

Alas!!
Sometimes I witness thundering waves, gushing and destroying ships.
Bellowing waves raging through hulls and masts adrift,
Wrecking thousands in dark and stormy seas
Angry Ocean's deathly blow, taking all down to the darkest depths.

I am the lighthouse, I only do my job.
My beacon steering all away from dangerous rocks;
Lost sailors veering in the rocky coasts and rugged seas in storm
The light is what they need to reach the docks

I stand tall, to clear away the misty darkness,
Navigating, seafarers the pathway in the sea's vastness
'Show us the lighthouse', they pray,
A heaven, an angel for travelers they say!!

I smile in the distance far away in pride,
I cannot sleep till my work is done to guide
Come, join me O' traveler just for a while,
Listen to the tales of travelers from far and wide.

I am so weary and tired, my body aches,
Standing for centuries awake;
Oh!!! But I cannot perish.
I am the lighthouse,
Standing strong through sleepless nights,
With memories of lives saved, to cherish.

'Oh, there comes another ship!!
I must shine to help the passerby….'

Daniel Moreschi is a poet from Neath, South Wales, United Kingdom. After life was turned upside down by his ongoing battle with severe M.E., he rediscovered his passion for poetry that had been dormant since his teenage years. Writing has served as a distraction from his struggles ever since. Daniel has been acclaimed by many poetry competitions, including the annual ones hosted by The Oliver Goldsmith Literature Festival, Wine Country Writers Festival, Short Stories Unlimited, Michigan Poetry Society, Ohio Poetry Day, Anansi Archive, Westmoreland Arts and Heritage Festival, and Inchicore Ledwidge Society. Daniel has also had poetry published by The Society of Classical Poets.

The Simmering Sea

Although the sea is pulled by lunar reins,
its servile ebbs conceal its subtle strides
towards a plot, once nature's patience wanes,
to test its tether with unruly tides.

As frozen hills are stoked by metal fumes
it brings a rhythmic ruse; a rippled grace,
while thriving swirls are topped by sprightly spumes,
that leads a charge when growing flows retrace.

And while humanity ignores the signs
of battered banks as billows belch and roar,
a steep caress erodes the coastal lines
and razes borders, like a siege of war.

Uprisings of tsunamis stir the straits
and garner fateful sways of ancient scales
till wayward spans cascade at mankind's gates.
A ceaseless song of simmered spite prevails.

When swept-up crowds are pleading for an ark
and lands are swallowed by the famished surge,
the moonlit sanctuaries turn to dark
as nature's wrath unfurls her final scourge.

Previously published in Michigan Poetry Society's Peninsula Poets: Contest Edition Fall 2022, after winning a 1st place award in their annual contest in the summer of 2022; the Spill Words journal on February 5th, 2023 https://spillwords.com/the-simmered-sea/, and Anansi Archive on January 3rd 2023, after placing 1st in the poetry category of their Winter 22/23 literary contest. https://www.anansiarchive.co.uk/waves-awake-by-daniel-moreschi/

Loralyn Sandoval De Luna is a guest lecturer at the College of Teacher Education in Batangas State University-The National Engineering University JPLPC Malvar, Philippines. She finished her Doctor of Philosophy in Educational Management degree in 2019 while teaching in Thailand and has edited and written for creative publications under Muang Thong Thani Adventist International Church. She also previously headed the Publications Committee of Bangkok Advent School, Thailand. Aside from being an educator, she plays the piano and the cello with her musician friends in church. She also enjoys watering garden plants, watching television dramas, and reading.

Sea of Tears

I have always dreamed of water
Still, I fear the vast unknown
I have never felt the tides of dawn
yet I know of sorrows drowned.

I have always dreamed of water
There I lay in deepest sea
I have never seen the angry waves
The dark and blue lay trapped in me.

I have never dreamed tomorrow
Of light and lovely bows
Know I've always dreamed of water,
I float, then sunk the lowest low.

Mark A. Fisher is a writer, poet, and playwright living in Tehachapi, California. His poetry has appeared in: *Reliquiae*, *Silver Blade*, *Eccentric Orbits*, and many other places. He was nominated for a Pushcart Prize for his poem "papyrus" in 2016. His first chapbook, *drifter*, is available from Amazon. His poem "there are fossils" (originally published in *Silver Blade*) came in second in the 2020 Dwarf Stars Speculative Poetry Competition. His plays have appeared on California stages in Pine Mountain Club, Tehachapi, Bakersfield, and Hayward. He has also won cooking ribbons at the Kern County Fair.

blue

the ocean spreads in its expanse
waves washing against stone and sand
the sun low and sanguine on the horizon
while the evening tide flows away

waves washing against stone and sand
the land breeze pulling romantics
while the evening tide flows away
away from the star filled sky

the land breeze pulling romantics
out onto empty lonely beaches
away from the star filled sky
their dreams drifting above the surf

out onto empty lonely beaches
wrapped up in sorrow and blues
their dreams drifting above the surf
another desolate day fading

wrapped up in sorrow and blues
the sun low and sanguine on the horizon
another desolate day fading
the ocean spreads in its expanse

by the sea

ruin
upon
rocky cliff
above breakers
~~~~~

where once she did live
beautiful Annabelle Lee
now sleeping beside the sea
nevermore waking
~~~~~

dancing in dreams
about these
crumbled
halls
dusty
and trackless
filled with shadows
~~~~~

scrawling out from pens
in penumbral poetry
chanted like a rosary
into the darkness
~~~~~

as a prayer
directed to
unknown
gods
bearing
no solace
for my spirit
~~~~~
~~~~~

only showing me
my responsibility
my insensibility
to my own disgrace
~~~~~
haunting this waste
therein my
madness
lies
~~~~~

Image by Dimitris Vetsikas from Pixabay

Dr. Richard M. Bañez is a Filipino associate professor for the undergraduate and graduate teacher education programs at the Batangas State University JPLPC-Malvar Campus. As an educator, he is primarily interested in language and literature pedagogy that focuses on students' capacity to engage in dynamic curricular opportunities and experiences within the context of teaching and learning English as a Second Language (ESL). He also conducts studies on Educational Management particularly on the intricate roles of language in educational leadership and supervision, and other research topics central to educational innovations. Aside from being in the academe, he is also an aspiring literary artist whose works have appeared in selected volumes of *Covid-19 Pandemic Poems* by Cape Comorin Publisher, *Love Letters in Poetic Verse* and *Castles and Courtyards* by Southern Arizona Press, and *Spring Offensive* by CultureCult Press.

To the Queen of Tejano Music

Miles and miles away, on this oriental seashore, I stand,
Where waves kiss the sand, and lighthouses gleam the land.
Ages and ages, your melodies persist,
A symphony of the sea lingers in each song's gentle twist.

Your voice echoes over the tide,
Enchanting far-eastern shores, where hearts open wide.
With the rhythm of the waves, your music takes flight,
Guiding travelers lost at sea, towards a blissful sight.

As I dance to your tunes, the seashells join in,
Whispering melodies, where the ocean and dreams begin.
*Baila Conmigo**, they sing, as the seagulls take flight,
Weaving a tapestry of joy, under the moon's silver light.

Your songs, a lighthouse's beam, cutting through the mist,
Leading lost souls ashore, where love can't be dismissed.
Immortalized, your art, like shells adorning the sand,
Treasured by a *Captive Heart**, embraced by a promised land.

*Donde Quiera Que Estés**, wherever you may be,
Your spirit lingers on, like whispers in the sea.
*Bidi Bidi Bom Bom**, a rhythm of pure delight,
*Techno Cumbia**, swirling waves, dancing day and night.

Within those beats, I find freedom, I find life,
As *Como La Flor**, blooming wild, casting away strife.
*A Million To One** hearts, resonate with your sound,
Bound by *Your Only Love**, a love that knows no bound.

*Is It the Beat** that echoes in my soul so deep?
That *I Could Fall in Love**, in this moment, I keep.
Like a parent and a lover, your music soothes my soul,
*Missing My Baby**, yet your melodies make me whole.

So, I'll continue to dance, on this seashore I roam,
Playing your songs, building sand castles where dreams find a home.
Here in my room, where the sea's whispers reside,
*Dreaming of You**, forever by my side.

*All the footnotes in this text are titles of Selena Quintanilla's album *Dreaming of You*, which was released in 1995 by EMI Latin, following the tragic death of the beloved singer. The album includes a number of Selena's most popular hits, such as *Dreaming of You*, *I Could Fall in Love*, and *Techno Cumbia.*

Liberation by the Sea

To swim in your chosen direction,
Embracing the call of the sea,
Where life flows with the tide,
And dreams are set free.

Like the summer breeze upon the waves,
I wander aimlessly and true,
Embracing the mysteries that await,
On paths untouched, anew.

No longer burdened by deliverables,
Nor confined by ticking hands of time,
I celebrate this liberation,
In a realm where worries don't chime.

Once a captain of a mighty vessel,
Navigating mapped itineraries,
Bound by the pursuit of treasures,
And calculating life's miseries.

But you abandoned my grand plan,
Sailing for personal gain and desires,
Transforming my ship into a war vessel,
Luring me to fight amongst fiery pyres.

In honor of your hollow victory,
I relinquished my captain's reign,
For the sea does not demand battles,
And my spirit yearns for freedom's domain.

So, I embrace life on the shores,
Where the sea's embrace is profound,
Where the heart finds comfort and peace,
And a new purpose is found.

No longer tethered to a ship's decree,
I find joy in the ocean's gentle sway,
To live a life of true liberation,
Where the sea's spirit guides my way.

Image by skygirl from Pixabay

Cai Quirk (they/them or ey/em) is a trans and genderqueer multi-disciplinary artist who focuses on the intersection of gender diversity throughout history, its erasure, and contemporary reclamation and re*story*ation. Their self-portrait series '*Transcendence*' engages with connections between gender, mythology, and nature-based spirituality, and was published in March 2023 with Skylark Editions. Cai's work has been exhibited in thirteen states and four countries, and in 2022, Cai gave over sixty talks and workshops in conferences across America. In the spring of 2022 Cai received the *Minnie Jane Scholarship* and a four-month artist residency from the Pendle Hill Quaker Center, where they created the poetry series '*Beyond Pink and Blue*'. They received bachelor's degrees in music and photography from Indiana University. See more at caiquirk.com.

Pine Green and Ocean Blue

pine needles and ocean waves
twine in shining tendrils just under my skin
ink growing and blossoming
flowing without a thought
more engrained than the blood in my veins

an apple tree is calling me, teaching me
branches intertwining with my pine teacher
another being who cycles and changes
flowers blooming and petals falling
fruits swelling and seeds sprouting

flowers and fruits sprout under my skin
interlaced with waves and pine boughs
tears flowing over new inked marks
another ordeal has left me breathless
but the spirits are pleased with my learning

these marks are my place, my identity
revealing my ordeals and challenges
gifted by spirit guides and teachers
more important even than family
or my physical body underneath

the sacred marks are our lifeline
lest our breath be snatched away
by winter wind or desert sands
our spirit-guides travel with us
embedded in skin, protecting

only those covered entirely in rippling forms
can seek the whole earth as a teacher
such wise sages must be fluid and supple
ebbing and flowing as ze does
to learn from zir great power and survive

the earth encompasses a flurry of shifts
forces of nature no human can change
seasons and ages, volcanoes and tidal waves
hurricanes swirling across zir skin
as ze dances spirals around the sun

I hope one day to be a wise sage
to be a student of the very earth zirself
but for now it is a simple blessing
to learn from beings already far wiser than me
pines, ocean waves, and apple trees

Image by Thanh Nguyen from Pixabay

Dr. Romel M. Aceron holds a Doctor of Philosophy in English Language Studies. He serves as the Research Coordinator of the College of Industrial Technology, Batangas State University JPLPC Malvar, Philippines. He has been teaching English language and literature courses in more than a decade. Dr. Aceron, serves as Research Coordinator of the College, and became the Head of External Affairs and Internationalization in the Campus. He is also a member and reviewer of various international research journals; editor-in-chief of the *Journal for Industrial Technology, Education, and Management*; curriculum planner and designer, book author-editor; Member of American Association of University Supervisors, Coordinators, and Directors of Language Programs. and a resource speaker.

Sea-son, The Bamboo House

Calling him upstairs, but still on a matted bamboo floor
While still lying on bed, tears falling—
Looking for a missing piece of heart;
Longing every single day like baby chicks
And many times, looking for a warmer weather
Burning out from wet and gloomy day.

Walking the street, seeing the old with a long gray hair
Going to another street, where patient's family have been waiting
And then another day, very silent little boy in the house—
Listening the sounds as thumbling and dancing waves of the sea
Dancing in a melody, along with the claps of the teens
Letting the pigeons fly high and reach the sky

New life new blessing,
Feeling the cool breeze of air with soup tomatoed fresh fish on a
bowl
Blessed to have her—gentle and caring;
Going near the sea, discovering what the world it could be
Finding the ways, people pulling the rope of the fishnet
Voices coming loud, enjoying and laughing

Exciting to go once more; finding new things at the sea
On the beat and rhythm of their feet—pulling and pulling the
rope
Amazing gold, silver, and diamond thumbling from the net
As men and women keep on picking them,
Putting them on the pale and sack,
Cheering and yelling as millionaire's flight

Running with other kids, but still unknown as tourist in a place
But, just making the self-familiar by picking the white stone and sand
Living in a barrio with loving and caring old seems not familiar,
But feeling the love since the first time it was,
Then, playing hide and seek, and running on very fine and soft sands
Transferring from house to house through passing under the bamboo floor.

Getting mad, with a loud but hasky voice,
Drunk with a wine from coconut juice cultured at top of the tree
Telling, don't be afraid little boy he is just drunk.
Keeping life as beautiful near the sea,
With full of love and care that could never fade
Inspiring to have the old like her love to people in the barrio,

Giving first aid care when sick and lost.
Playing with, in sounding waves of the sea,
Reminding of how simple and beautiful the life could be
As hearts lend and care as treasure of the past.
No one can compare, just old woman but able to keep you safe
With basic needs, respect, love, and care as family.

Refreshing and sweating, enjoying with them,
But once again calling for lunch is ready, but dreaming
Feeling the love and care of mother on her behalf
As comforting flows in veins, heart and soul
Forgetting her is like suicide and a mafia—tears in heaven
She lost far, and never seen, as young little boy weak, but the memories and love remain

Paul Gilliland retired after over 30 years of service with the US Army and settled in the high desert of Southeast Arizona, just miles from the historic wild west towns of Tombstone and Bisbee. He holds Associate of Applied Science Degrees in Intelligence Studies, Linguistics, and Education from Cochise College; a Bachelor of Arts Degree in Music Theory/Composition and Technical Theater Design from Olivet College; and a Master of Fine Arts Degree in Music Composition from the Vermont College of Fine Arts. He is an educator, composer of 21st century chamber music, author, form poet, and publisher. He is a member of the American Society of Composers, Authors, and Publishers (ASCAP); National Writers Union; Authors Guild; Poetry Society of America; the Academy of American Poets; and the Association for Publishers for Special Sales. In addition to teaching interviewing techniques and report writing for the US Army, he is the Editor-in-Chief of his own publishing company, Southern Arizona Press. He currently has three published volumes of poetry, *Hindsights of 2020*, *The Journey of the Fool: A Poetic Journey in Three Parts*, and *A Heroic Crown and Other Sonnets*, all available through Amazon. He is currently working on completing his fourth collection of poetry, *Tales from a Southwest Inn.* His poetry appears online in numerous Facebook poetry group as well as being published in *Sonnet Sanctuary Anthology Volume 1* (A Romeo Nation), *Open Skies Quarterly Volumes 4, 5, 6, Perceptions, Dark Reflections*, and *Myths, Legends, and Lore* (Shrouded Eye Press), and *From Sunset to Sunrise* (Dark Poetry Society Anthology). When not busy with teaching, reading, editing, and publishing, he provides services as a Certified Expert Sound Healer.

He can be followed online at:

https://www.facebook.com/PaulGillilandPoetry
https://www.facebook.com/SouthernArizonaPress
http://www.PaulGillilandMusic.com/
https://www.SouthernArizonaPress.com/

The Blue Grotto

The north side of the island
Has a cavern by the sea
Once thought the home of witches
And the monsters of Capri

But people came to visit
Its luminescent hue
And tourist started flocking
To see the Grotto Blue

When sea and waves are tranquil
And tides remaining low
The boatman has you watch your head
And in the cave you go

Now inside the grotto
A mystic glow is seen
The azure of the water
Aglow with diamond sheen

And so now when you visit
The Island of Capri
You know which hidden grotto's
The one you want to see

The Curse of the Unsinkable Stoker

At the dawn of the twentieth century
A youth born by the sea
Was drawn to the water's edge
With a fate he could not foresee

The life of Arthur Priest
Who was known to his friends as Jack
Would lead to the death of many
For the curse upon his back

He was lured by the sounds of the Sirens
And the beautiful songs they sang
And by the time that he was twenty
He was part of a ships "black gang"

For in the deepest bowels
Of ships all powered by coal
Jack Priest would sing the Siren's songs
That seduced his younger soul

The fate of the Siren's would call the ship
But each time he was spared
And thus, each ship that he would board
Was by the curse ensnared

The Asturias was the first
Vessel he would embark
And on its maiden voyage
A collision left its mark

The Sirens showed some mercy
As no man was lured to doom
And thus, a simple accident
Was what maritime would assume

Next was the Olympic
The largest liner on the sea
But on its fifth voyage
Was a collision blamed on thee

For as it made a starboard turn
The Hawke was sucked off course
Which struck her in the starboard side
With devastating force

Again no one was taken
By the Sirens of the deep
But the Olympic was found guilty
And her repairs did not come cheap

So, seven short months later
The Titanic had set sail
With Jack deep in the engine room
And thus, a change in tale

For in the dark of night
As Jack shoveled coal below
The ship hit an iceberg
That caused a massive blow

The ship began to flounder
To sink was a guarantee
And in less than three hours
It slipped beneath the sea

The Sirens now were ready
As fifteen hundred met their doom
Into the north Atlantic
That would now become their tomb

But Jack, the faithful stoker
Was rescued from the deep
To sail on future vessels
As his life he would keep

The liner Alcantara
Was the next ship that he charmed
But at the start of World War One
The cruiser was then armed

In February, nineteen sixteen
It battled a German ship
With damage that was so severe
It caused the ship to flip

For once again the Sirens
Had taken back their due
For three hundred men aboard the ships
Would not live to see it through

But our dear Jack was listed
Among those that had survived
And so, he was enlisted
On another when he arrived

So now aboard Britannic
From White Star's Olympic fleet
A refitted floating hospital
Bound for the Isles near Crete

On twenty-one November
An explosion shook the ship
Again, to the starboard side
The vessel began to tip

The captain steered Britannic
In an attempt to run aground
Then ordered all the lifeboats
To be prepared so no one drowned

But the crew lowered lifeboats
In a panicked state of wits
Two were sucked into the props
And quickly chopped to bits

Now once again our stoker Jack
Had found his life intact
While thirty men had lost their life
As part of the attack

Another of the survivors
On the ship that faithful day
Was the nurse named Violet Jessop
Who like Jack had seen a stay

For Violet, just like Jack
Had been aboard the White Star ships
Both Olympic and Titanic
When they made their faithful trips

The final ship that Jack would sail
Was the SS Donegal
That sunk in the English Channel
When a torpedo hit its hull

Now forty men met their maker
All on that faithful day
The Sirens once again had come
To take their souls away

A final ship survivor
From White Star shipwreck fame
Did not survive that ship's attack
Archie Jewell was his name

He had been aboard Titanic
And survived Britannic's end
But on the SS Donegal
It was death he would befriend

And so, the Stoker Arthur
Who was known to his friends as Jack
Would give up working on the seas
After this U-boat attack

He claimed no one would sail with him
There was a curse upon his back
For he will forever be known as
The Unsinkable Stoker, Jack

Castles on the Sand

The kings all built grand castles
But each was made of sand
Upon every kingdoms shore
Where oceans meet the land

They hosted gala banquets
Within these castle halls
But they refused to notice
How the sea wore down the walls

As they were busy drinking
Enjoying merriments
The waves of time came crashing
To erode the battlements

'Til finally in delirium
The sea burst in a squall
And as the tide began to ebb
The ramparts all would fall

Each king stood by his castle
Deferred to set it free
As they watch all their morning work
Get washed back to the sea

Gone Without a Trace

One's life must be worth living, every day we do our best
Our thoughts and dreams are shared and our opinions are
expressed
We try to make an impact on those people all around
With hopes that in our later years our names will be renowned

But often we go daily with so few that recognize
The simple gestures that are made before their very eyes

As artists, authors, poets, we create despite the cost
In hopes that in the future all our work will not be lost
Like footsteps on the beaches that the wind and waves erase
Our artistry may in the end be gone without a trace

The Lonely Lighthouse Keepers

On far off distant rocky crags
Are single lights aglow
To warn the mariners at sea
Of spots they shall not go

When late at night the fog grows thick
And covers up the light
The sailors listen for the horns
That sound throughout the night

The lonely men who keep the light
And nightly sound the horn
Are saviors for the men at sea
Until the break of morn

Although they live a simple life
And many live alone
The thanks they get from sailor men
Is thanks that's never shown

A Storm Brewing at Sea

The lonely lighthouse keeper watches west from top his keep
For miles he sees the calming waves upon the vast blue deep
Where setting sun reflects upon the sea like diamonds cast
And ships and boats of every size are slowly sailing past

But as the weather changes and the sea begins to rise
He sees the dark clouds brewing up a storm before his eyes

He goes into the lantern room and focuses the light
To warn the ships of dangers near the cliffs throughout the night
He powers up the foghorn so to keep them all at bay
And knows they will be safe until tomorrow's break of day

Waves Against the Shore

The waves of time each lap against the sand
As morning's sun sends rays to break the dawn
The ebbing tide retreats away from land
Until the flowing streams are all but gone

The sands of time are born from jagged cliffs
That face the sea defiantly with grace
For as the waves maintain their rhythmic riffs
They slowly wash the grains from on its face

Crescendos of the surf come with the storms
While freezing winds provide some added aid
Eroding rock gives way to newer forms
Til even newer forms begin to fade

The waves continue beating at the shore
Until the rocky cliffs are there no more

The Waves at Sea

The waves at sea
Each reach the shore in rhythmic dance.
The waves at sea
With surf and foam that's flowing free
Seduces us with its romance
And binds us in a sacred trance
The waves at sea

The Secret of the Sea

(Acrostic Quote)

Would it be helmsmen shanties
You heard across the sea
To ***learn*** the haunting melody
Of ***the*** requiem set free
The ***secret*** understanding
Of ships lost into the deep
The spirits of the sailors
In eternal ***sea*** bed's sleep

Only memories remain
Of ***those*** of flesh and bone
Who set out on their voyages
To ***brave*** the great unknown
It's now because of these lost souls
And ***dangers*** that they faced
We ***comprehend*** the ocean
With ***its mysteries*** embraced

Would you learn the secret of the sea? Only those who brave its dangers, comprehend its mystery." – Henry Wadsworth Longfellow – The Secret of the Sea (1850)

Previous anthologies from Southern Arizona Press

The Stars and Moon in the Evening Sky is a collection of 120 poetic works crafted by 65 poets from across the globe inspired by the universe around us.

Dragonflies and Fairies is a collection of 72 poetic works crafted by 34 poets from across the globe celebrating the magical and mystical creatures of folklore.

Ghostly Ghouls and Haunted Happenings is a collection of 129 poetic works crafted by 46 poets from across the globe inspired by ghosts, ghouls, and things that go bump in the night.

The Poppy: A Symbol of Remembrance examines the history of the poppy as a flower of remembrance, over 80 poems and lyrics written by World War One poets between 1912 and 1925, and 79 poems written by 21st Century poets from around the globe in remembrance of the fallen heroes from all war of the last century.

The Wonders of Winter is a collection of 120 poetic works crafted by 50 poets from across the globe that celebrate the winter season.

Love Letters in Poetic Verse is a collection of 143 poetic works written and contributed by 58 poets from across the globe celebrating romance and love.

Castles and Courtyards is a collection of 79 poetic works written and contributed by 37 poets from across the globe celebrating the medieval life of Kings, Queens, peasants, and troubadours.

***Poetry Inspired by "A Midsummer Night's Dream*"** is a collection of 102 poems penned by 43 bards from across the globe inspired by William Shakespeare's romantic comedy *A Midsummer Night's Dream.*

Upcoming anthologies from Southern Arizona Press

The Children's Book of Bedtime Verse – A collection of poetic works appropriate for reading to children at bedtime. Coming in early October 2023.

Home for the Holidays – A holiday anthology of poetic works celebrating the gathering of family during the fall and winter holidays. Coming in early December 2023.

Poets interested in submitting works for upcoming anthologies are asked to check out our Current Submissions page at: http://www.southernarizonapress.com/current-submissions/ for more information about each anthology and our process for submission.

New independent releases from Southern Arizona Press

April Verses by Dibyasree Nandy. Getting up early in the morning, savouring the clemency of the month, at the threshold of a severe summer, we turn to poetry as the means to paint a picture of the mountains and seas.

https://www.amazon.com/dp/1960038273

Removing Interference: From Words of Life by Courtenay Nold - As I started reading *Removing Interference*, I realized that Courtenay's work was what I needed in my life. So often, I get pulled in different directions, and remaining who I was became challenging. Her poetry brought me to a time when I approached life with wonder because there was less, by less - I mean less worry, stress, and anxiety about things I could not control. As I moved through her work, I found a sense of calm or an oasis - if you will - in the desert of life: A place where I could renew my spirit to face life's challenges. I hope you can take some time, fill your coffee cup, and read in a way that makes *From Words of Life* more than a tagline. She has written from her life experiences and has brought them into our lives in ways few others could. Thank you, Courtenay, for this honor.
- Travis Partington: Oscar Mike Radio Podcast; www.oscarmikeradio.com

https://www.amazon.com/dp/1960038303

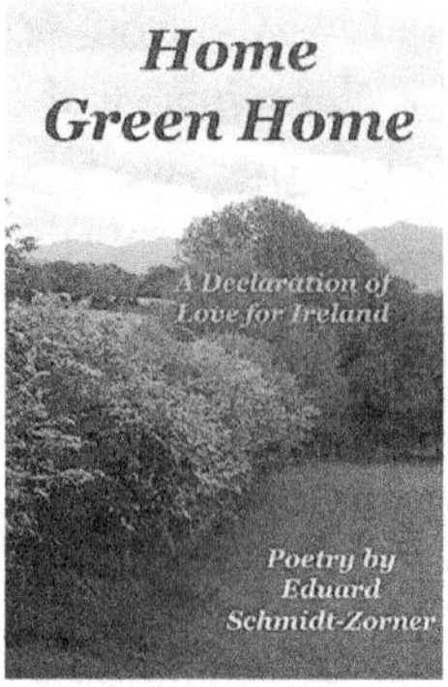

Home Green Home: A Declaration of Love for Ireland - Eduard Schmidt-Zorner is a translator and writer of poetry, haibun, haiku and short stories. He writes in four languages: English, French, Spanish, and German. He also writes under his pen name: Eadbhard McGowan. He is a member of four writer groups in Ireland and has lived in County Kerry, Ireland, for more than 30 years and is a proud Irish citizen, born in Germany. He is published in over 200 anthologies, literary journals and broadsheets in the USA, UK, Ireland, Australia, Canada, Japan, Sweden, Spain, Italy, France, Austria, Bangladesh,

https://www.amazon.com/dp/196003829X

Nature Photographer Bob Collins has spent the last 25 years traveling and photographing ***The Magic of an Upper Peninsula Autumn***. In this book, Bob not only shares some of his marvelous autumn photographs, but provides information on planning and executing your own discovery of Michigan's Upper Peninsula as the fall colors begin to turn. Complete with detailed driving instructions, grid coordinates and points of interest, Bob has made navigating Michigan's Upper Peninsula as easy as it can be. Enjoy his photographs and make plans to visit and experience Michigan's Upper Peninsula on your own.

https://www.amazon.com/dp/1960038281

Poet, novelist, and long-time radio enthusiast T.D. Walker has written a book that speaks to the crisis of our time. Forged during the COVID lockdown when citizens were both terrified of contagion yet newly unified by extremity, these poignant verses invite us to consider how language shapes the menaces around us whether it might be the casualties of the 1982 Falkland War, the 1986 nuclear disaster of Chernobyl, or "how many ways there are to destroy the earth." Weaving together many strands from her specialized knowledge -- for example, references about HAARP, high frequency radio waves, ionospheric heating, and the Shortwave Transmissions Project -- ***Doubt & Circuitry*** is always bristling with verbal energy and unexpected turns in strong, limber lines. Essential reading.

https://www.amazon.com/dp/196003832X

In an inspired re-visiting of Old Testament stories, Kenneth Robbins brings these tales to life, capturing their spirit (and a bit of the Spirit) with vivid poetry and unfettered imagination. The seed of the ancient language is allowed to bloom, revealing to the reader new and deeper meanings obscured in the original. Revelatory, often gut-wrenching, with humorous curveballs, ***The Book of Sorrows*** is a powerful plea for the understanding of existence.

https://www.amazon.com/dp/1960038338

Individuals interested in working with Southern Arizona Press to bring their books to print are asked to review our publishing services at:

https://www.southernarizonapress.com/publish-with-us/

Published works by our featured contributors

Love Poems for Michael by Joan McNerney
Many reflect on New England with autumn foliage and fierce winters. However, four seasons do include bursting springs and boiling summers. Love is its own season, its own country, its own domain. Let's explore love up north during spring and summer.

https://www.amazon.com/Love-Poems-Michael-Joan-McNerney/dp/9388319656
https://www.cyberwit.net/publications/1602

At Work by Joan McNerney explores everyday workers. It is unique because each worker, either female or male, receives their own page. These are snapshots of people who are either content with or made unhappy by their daily circumstances. Reading this book is an exploration of human nature at its core.

https://www.amazon.com/At-Work-Joan-McNerney/dp/8182537835

https://www.cyberwit.net/publications/1759

The Muse in Miniature by Joan McNerney
There is no doubt this poet very aptly traverses an immense range of emotion and experience. Here we find poetry's passion and powerful imagination in rich abundance.

https://www.amazon.com/Muse-Miniature-Joan-McNerney/dp/9389074509

https://www.cyberwit.net/publications/1262

Fireflies Beneath the Misty Moon is a collection of Ekphrastic poems written by Dibyasree Nandy inspired by the works of Japanese artists Okumura Masanobu, Suzuki Harunobu, Utagawa Kunisada, Yoshitoshi Tsukioka, Kobayashi Kiyochika, Ogata Gekko, Toshikata Mizuno, Settai Komura, Torii Kotondo, and Kondo Shiun.
A Southern Arizona Press Published Book.

https://www.amazon.com/dp/1960038125

In her debut collection, ***The World Eats Love***, Carol Edwards interlaces a narrative of characters bearing up under the weight of longing, loss, and regret. She unfolds, with reassuring tenderness, a spectrum of experiences: from stolen innocence to wasted time; from insidious monsters to bittersweet loneliness; from the heaviness of broken hearts to the hope of belonging. She concludes with a short story—a fairy tale, of sorts—to capture in prose themes woven throughout the poems.

https://www.amazon.com/dp/064578561X

Poems and Micropoems is the newest collection of 80 haiku, 44 tanka, and 35 longer poems by Indian English poet Ram Krishna Singh, who is a creative genius of many excellences.
A Southern Arizona Press Published Book.

https://www.amazon.com/dp/1960038087

Aequilateralis - "Possessing a unique voice, Ken Allan Dronsfield has lured many a reader into his world of word play with his prolific writing on a wide range of subjects, but mainly his poetry relating to nature truly takes my breath away. He has the ability to reach a diverse audience; and he touches the heart and mind of all who enter the pages of his expressive and imagery-filled poetry books. After reading silently several times, I decide to read each poem out loud, words tumbling smoothly from my lips cascading down onto the previous, which then turn the experience into a theatrical realm with marked acts as if a play, enhancing this extremely entertaining book even more so than what the already brilliant command of his language usage had caught our attention with, in the first place." - Leslie De Luca, Canada.

A Southern Arizona Press Published Book.

https://www.amazon.com/dp/1960038117

The publisher Cyberwit.net released the first paperback poetry collection of Nolo Segundo titled ***The Enormity of Existence*** in 2020 and has since published two more collections: ***Of Ether and Earth*** [2021] and ***Soul Songs*** [2022]. These titles and many of the poems in the books reflect the awareness the poet gained when he had an NDE (near-death experience) when he almost drowned at 24 in the Winooski River in Vermont: That he has--IS--a consciousness that predates birth and survives death, what poets since Plato have called the soul. For 52 years he's had more questions than answers, but knows this world is really just a dream, seeming 'real' until you 'awaken'-- much like you do every morning.

https://www.cyberwit.net/publications/1532

Cai Quirk's ***Transcendence: Queer Restoryation*** invites people into a world where distinctions of gender, time, and place become fluid and flexible. Binary ways of seeing the world will not simply disappear — we must actively replace them. 38 self-portrait photographs and six mythic tales explore paths beyond supposed binaries, creating new stories that empower, inspire, and heal. The book came out this spring with Skylark Editions

https://www.skylarkeditions.org/shop/pre-order-transcendence-queer-restoryation

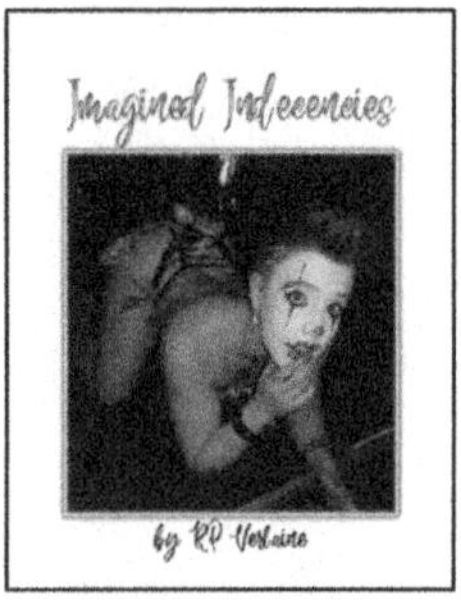

Imagined Indecencies is Rp Verlaine's third book. Poetry that is Profusely Illustrated with color photos taken by Verlaine of models and friends who posed for him. The poems are haiku, Seneru, sonnets, and one-line poems. A notable change from previous books is there are several free verse poems as well. All the poems have been published before in Literary Journals, Magazines, Newspapers, and websites. They have been published in Japan, Africa, Wales, Scotland and of course Verlaine's native America.

https://www.amazon.com/Imagined-Indecencies-Rp-Verlaine/dp/145663867X

MacKenzie Publishing published its third anthology, ***No One Should Kiss a Frog*** in 2023. Fiction, non-fiction, and poetry from 75 authors around the world writing to the theme of "love gone wrong."

A frog never turns into a prince (no words can mince that fact), and odds are highly stacked that frogs don't turn into princesses wearing fancy dresses...

https://www.amazon.com/dp/199058912X

Fragrance of Love is the first book of poetry by Anil Kumar Panda.

https://www.amazon.in/Fragrance-Love-Anil.../dp/9352072820

Melody of Love is the second book of poetry by Anil Kumar Panda mainly centered on love and life that fill readers mind with a sweet aroma of young love.

https://www.amazon.in/dp/B073TTQ4J4

Poetry to Tasneem Hossain is an ever-flowing river reflecting all that surrounds us. ***The Pearl Necklace*** is a lyrical journey of sensitivity and contemplation through life in its different colors and shades. The title poem is about unfulfilled true love. *The Invisible cord* is a celebration of mother's love. *Agony* is a cry for social justice. The last poem *The lighthouse* ends with an aspiration to make our existence more meaningful. The essence of her poems is the beauty of nature and human life.

https://forms.gle/4JdcJi792ZSZS63R7

The poems of Tasneem Hossain's ***Floating Feathers*** are an outcome of the spiraling moments of her emotional outbursts. The poem *Floating Feathers* is a confession of the poetic thoughts floating and falling into her lap. *Let's walk together, you and I* deals with old age agonies and pains of becoming senile. Human emotions, social justice, kindness towards humanity and transience of life are some of the themes of her poetry. At the end there is a collection of haiku poems.

https://forms.gle/4JdcJi792ZSZS63R7

Tasneem Hossain's book ***Split and Splice*** is a compilation of some of the writer's articles published in different newspapers. Some of the articles deal with historical events and interesting facts about different issues, some are about acquiring good habits for a peaceful and successful life, some discuss ways of improving lifestyles and overall well-being having relevance to day-to-day life. The different aspects of life will help readers to become more conscious of life and the world surrounding them.

https://forms.gle/4JdcJi792ZSZS63R7

Tasneem Hossain's book ***Grass in Green*** is a journey through life's different moments. In a world full of chaos and complexity the title poem *Grass in Green* speaks of harmony between communities, countries and religions leading to a life of happiness and peace. *Fractured: Rise* is about domestic abuse and courage to fight it. *I am a Prostitute* creates awareness in society. Greed and misuse of power is the theme of *Pawns in the Game.* Some of the poems portray the devastation created by COVID 19 ending on a note of hope; some are affirmations for gender equality; some express love in its purest form; some speak of the inevitable uncertainties of life and inspire us to recuperate; and be strong to embrace the inevitable changes and jump back to life again with vigour.
A Southern Arizona Press Published Book.

https://www.amazon.com/dp/1960038060

the last polar bear on earth by Rhian Elizabeth contains poems about being sick and being in love. finding out you've got a serious illness like multiple sclerosis is a bit like falling in love. you are never quite the same again. when you get your heartbroken, it's like getting the news that you're ill. It's a process of grief and you think your life is over and that you will never move on, but you do. alternatively, when you become ill and when you fall in love, you are just simply f***

https://www.amazon.co.uk/last-polar-bear-earth/dp/1912109476

Time for Verses by Eduard Schmidt-Zorner is a poetry collection, which was published by Cyberwit.net, deals with different aspects of life.

The poems included in this book show a wonderful wealth of original thought. The flights of the poet's imagination are quite impressive and remarkable.

We find here bold and new images. The poet with strong imagination is able to create the song of the soul in these poems.

https://www.amazon.com/TIME-VERSES-Eduard.../dp/8119228413